COIN HUNTING: RARE & ERROR UK COINS

What to look for in Change and Bank Bags

1st Edition

coinhunter

Index

Introduction

Welcome to the first edition of COIN HUNTING: RARE & ERROR UK COINS - What to look for in Change and Bank Bags.

This book describes coin error types and features other higher value coins that can be found in your change.

It is aimed at both experienced collectors and those with just a passing interest in coins.

What is Coin Hunting?

In its simplest form, Coin Hunting can be just checking your change for coins that look a bit different to what you would normally see.

It is possible to get hold of bags of coins from banks or the Post Office, more coins to check = more chance of finding something of value.

The section "Coin Hunting in 2024 and beyond" goes into more detail and offers advice to people who would like to check bags of coins to find designs missing from their collection.

What are Error Coins?

All UK coins are produced by The Royal Mint, mistakes do happen and any resulting coin that does not fall within an accepted tolerance of variation for mass produced coins, would be considered an error.

For more information, please see the "Is the coin actually an error?" section.

To understand coin errors, you must first understand how coins are minted. If you know the process, you know what errors are possible and importantly, those that are not.

After reading this book, you will be familiar with the processes used by The Royal Mint to create coins from sheets of metal. You will understand the types of UK decimal coin errors and know which ones are most desirable and valuable.

Error Coin Values

As with any coin, the price that can be attained at a point in time depends on the buyers interested in your coin.

In this book a guide price range is shown for each error coin type, the range relates to most sales of the type shown, but there will be very special examples that achieve higher prices at auction.

The guide price range is often wide due to variations in error severity and limited sales records for some UK decimal error coin types.

Many error coins have unique elements and a few are absolutely unique. This makes individual coin valuation very difficult, so the auction route is a popular one for error coins, where they can find their value on the day based on competitive bidding.

What are "rare" Royal Mint coins?

There are a number of normal UK coins with no errors that command prices significantly above face value, normally based primarily on rarity.

No coin in circulation today is truly rare, even the lowest mintage circulation coins can only be considered comparatively rare or "rarer than other coins".

To help you know which coins to look out for above all others, this book includes a "Top 20 Most Valuable Circulation Coins" list – they are all comparatively rare, mintage figures are shown for each coin where available.

From Start to Finish?

The topics in this book are presented in an order that would suit most coin collectors, with the minting process at the start along with clarification of what would and would not be considered an error on UK coins.

The middle of the book describes Error Coin Types in some detail, with images to help you understand what some errors of the type might look like. Whilst more severe coin errors may be immediately obvious, there are a number of more subtle errors. This section will help you spot and identify them when Coin Hunting.

Some people may wish to use the Error Coin section as a reference to refer back to, if you wish to skip on to the Coin Hunting section. The book will still make sense, just look back to find out more when specific coin errors that can be found in change are referenced.

If you're new to coin collecting, it is recommended that you have a quick look at the "Glossary of Terms and Abbreviations" to get a little more familiar with some of the "coin language" used in this book.

Understanding error coins can seem like a daunting task, I have tried to clearly explain each error without unnecessary jargon. If you are new to error coins, take a bit of extra time reading "The Royal Mint - Modern Minting" and "Is the coin actually an error?" sections, as these will give you the foundation information needed to build your UK error coin knowledge. I hope you enjoy reading this book.

Expert Grading for
the World of Collectibles.

Coin authentication,
grading & encapsulation

NGCcoin.uk

Paper money authentication
grading & encapsulation

PMGnotes.uk

Comic book authentication,
grading & encapsulation

CGCcomics.uk

Card authentication,
grading & encapsulation

CGCcards.uk

Top 20 Most Valuable Circulation Coins

Card colour indicates rarity based on circulation mintage figures published by The Royal Mint. Coin sales as Brilliant Uncirculated (BU) or Uncirculated (UNC) mintage figures are also shown.

Mintage	Mintage	Mintage	Mintage	Mintage	Mintage
<100,000	100k-250k	250k-500k	500k-1m	1m-1.5m	>1.5m

£140

Kew Gardens

Year of Issue: 2009
Mintage: Circulation **210,000**
Reverse: Christopher Le Brun
BU Mintage: 128,364

£32

Commonwealth Games - Northern Ireland

Year of Issue: 2002
Mintage: Circulation **485,500**
Reverse: Matthew Bonaccorsi
BU Mintage: 18,812
Edge: SPIRIT OF FRIENDSHIP,MANCHESTER 2002

£13

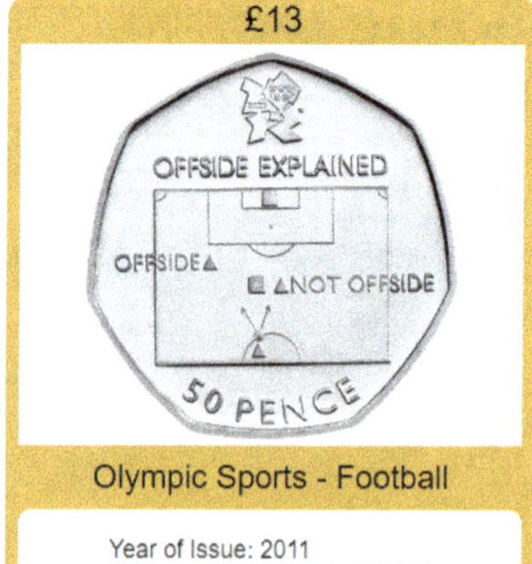

Olympic Sports - Football

Year of Issue: 2011
Mintage: Circulation **1,125,500**
Reverse: Neil Wolfson
UNC Mintage: 188,262

£13

Commonwealth Games - Wales

Year of Issue: 2002
Mintage: Circulation **588,500**
Reverse: Matthew Bonaccorsi
BU Mintage: 18,812
Edge: SPIRIT OF FRIENDSHIP,MANCHESTER 2002

£12.50

A - Angel of the North

Year of Issue: 2019
Mintage: Circulation **84,000**
Reverse: Dave Knapton
UNC Mintage: 29,908

£10.50

Olympic Sports - Triathlon

Year of Issue: 2011
Mintage: Circulation **1,163,500**
Reverse: Sarah Harvey
UNC Mintage: 146,354

£10

A - Angel of the North

Year of Issue: 2018
Mintage: Circulation **220,000**
Reverse: Dave Knapton
UNC Mintage: 156,704

£10

Olympic Sports - Judo

Year of Issue: 2011
Mintage: Circulation **1,161,500**
Reverse: David Cornell
UNC Mintage: 128,442

£10

Commonwealth Games - England

Year of Issue: 2002
Mintage: Circulation **650,500**
Reverse: Matthew Bonaccorsi
BU Mintage: 18,812
Edge: SPIRIT OF
FRIENDSHIP,MANCHESTER 2002

£8.50

B - Bond... James Bond

Year of Issue: 2019
Mintage: Circulation **84,000**
Reverse: Lee Jones
UNC Mintage: 29,005

Commonwealth Games - Scotland

Year of Issue: 2002
Mintage: Circulation **771,750**
Reverse: Matthew Bonaccorsi
BU Mintage: 18,812
Edge: SPIRIT OF
FRIENDSHIP,MANCHESTER 2002

Y - Yeoman Warder

Year of Issue: 2019
Mintage: Circulation **63,000**
Reverse: The Royal Mint Team
UNC Mintage: 28,003

R - Robin

Year of Issue: 2019
Mintage: Circulation **64,000**
Reverse: The Royal Mint Team
UNC Mintage: 29,173

Olympic Sports - Wrestling

Year of Issue: 2011
Mintage: Circulation **1,129,500**
Reverse: Roderick Enriquez
UNC Mintage: 127,279

Z - Zebra Crossing

Year of Issue: 2019
Mintage: Circulation **63,000**
Reverse: P J Lynch
UNC Mintage: 27,076

Jemima Puddle-Duck

Year of Issue: 2016
Mintage: Circulation **2,100,000**
Reverse: Emma Noble
BU Mintage: 138,937

All these coins entered UK circulation and could still be found in your change today. There are error coins worth more than the coins shown here, but only "Non Error Coins" are included in this list.

The Royal Mint - Modern Minting

The process described applies to modern UK decimal coins struck for circulation, there are differences in production for the Brilliant Uncirculated quality coins used for coin sets and packs.

The Royal Mint start the process as they have for over a millennium, by melting down metal in a furnace.

Creating Blanks

In modern times, the alloys created such as cupronickel are rolled into sheets of the correct thickness for the coin blanks required.

Discs of metal (or other coin shapes) are then punched from the strip by a blanking press. The press can make up to 10,000 discs a minute. These are called blanks or planchets.

Rolling metal under great pressure makes it hard, so the next thing to do is soften the metal in an annealing furnace at temperatures of about 500°C. The blanks are then cleaned using chemicals and ball bearings to make sure there are no marks or blemishes.

Creating a Master Die

An engraving machine uses a digital file to cut the design into a piece of steel that is the size of the final coin. This is known as a "reduction punch" and will be used to make the dies that actually strike the coins.

For the final part of the process, the blanks are tipped into a hopper at the top of a coining press that contains a pair of dies.

Applying a pressure of around 60 tonnes, the dies strike the blanks and turn them into coins at speeds of about 750 strikes a minute.

Currently The Royal Mint have 27 coining presses, so could potentially produce over 20,000 coins a minute, which is more than 300 per second.

Many of the UK decimal coin errors come about during blank creation and storage, with some of the more spectacular errors being initiated at the coin feed stage of the process.

Feed, Strike, Eject

A rotating wheel called a dial plate receives blanks and moves them into position between the dies, pushing the blank into a retaining collar against the upper die for striking. The wheel turns to eject the struck coin before receiving the next blank.

If the coin has a milled edge, the retaining collar creates the milled impression when the blank is struck between the two dies and the metal spreads outward.

Note: Whilst 50p blanks are shaped, 20p coin blanks are completely round, they are shaped entirely by the retaining collar during the striking process.

Quality Control

Two words that do not fit well with collecting UK error coins. Fortunately, the sheer scale and speed of production mean that errors will make it to the bagging process for circulation coins and to the packing process for Brilliant Uncirculated coins.

The 10 Most Publicised UK Coin Errors

These are the popular errors, the ones that have received press attention, most coin collectors know to look out for these coins.

They are a mixed bag in terms of value and rarity, you do have a realistic chance of finding some of these in change.

£50

Undated 20p (Error: Mule)

Year of Issue: 2008
Mintage: Circulation up to 250,000*
Reverse: Matthew Dent

*Royal Mint estimate

£800

1983 New Pence 2p (Error: Mule)

Year of Issue: 1983
UNC Mintage: 1,000 (estimate)
Reverse: Christopher Ironside

NOT STRUCK FOR CIRCULATION

£6

**First World War Centenary Navy
(Error: Cracked Die - "Flag")**

Year of Issue: 2015
Mintage: Circulation 20,000 (estimate)
Reverse: David Rowlands
Edge: THE SURE SHIELD OF BRITAIN

£25

**Shakespeare Tragedies
(Error: Edge Inscription)**

Year of Issue: 2016
Mintage: Circulation 15,000 (estimate)
Reverse: John Bergdahl
Edge: FOR KING AND COUNTRY

<table>
<tr><td>

£35

Benjamin Bunny (Error: Rotation 1 side)

Year of Issue: 2017
Mintage: Circulation 20,000 (estimate)
Reverse: Emma Noble

</td><td>

£1000

NO DENOMINATION

First World War Centenary (Error: Mule)

Year of Issue: 2014
Mintage: Circulation No Estimate, Very Scarce
Reverse: John Bergdahl
Edge: THE LAMPS ARE GOING OUT ALL OVER EUROPE

</td></tr>
<tr><td>

£60

Britannia (Error: Rotation up to 150")

Year of Issue: 2015
Mintage: Circulation 10,000 (estimate)
Reverse: Antony Dufort
Edge: QUATUOR MARIA VINDICO

</td><td>

£200

2016 / 2017 Dual Date £1 (Error: Mule)

Year of Issue: 2016
Mintage: Circulation No Estimate, Scarce
Reverse: David Pearce

</td></tr>
<tr><td>

£120

Nations of the Crown £1 (Error: Fried Egg)

Years of Issue: 2016-2022
Mintage: Circulation 5,000 (estimate)
Reverse: David Pearce

</td><td>

£250

Crowned English Rose 20p (Error: Wrong Planchet, Bronze)

Years of Issue: 1982-2008
Mintage: Circulation No Estimate, Very Scarce
Reverse: William Gardner

</td></tr>
</table>

Is the coin actually an error?

First of all, an imperfect coin, or one not like other versions of the same coin; is not necessarily a minting error.

Most of the coins we are asked to inspect fall into one of four categories, all of which are not genuine errors that occurred in production of the coin:

1: As intended but the public have been misled by incorrect information

Example: If the writing on the edge of the coin is "upside down" – this is just because the minting process strikes the edge lettering before the main design, so it can be either way up.

2: As intended but imperfect due to mass production

£2 Coin Example: Some dots on the heads side are missing or part of the design on the tails side is missing in the gap between the gold outer and the silver inner. This is just due to the speed of manufacture for circulation coins, there are countless minor imperfections that can never be considered errors.

Edge lettering, words not properly formed is another example of an imperfection not considered to be an error: The 1999 Rugby World Cup £2 coin often shows 999 as the year on the edge inscription, the 1 may look feint or appear to be missing.

Edge letter imperfections result from the methods used to add the edge inscription before the coin is struck. The inscription is rolled onto the edge of a coin using a machine that makes an impression into the metal – some parts may not have the same depth of impression and letter impressions could be incomplete.

Even when the impression is complete – it is still possible that certain letters and numbers such as I or 1 or parts of other letters such as the diagonal of a letter R can be "closed over" by the pressure of the striking process, as the edge metal flows into the retaining collar, especially if the impression was weak.

Just to make issues even more likely, the milled edge used for £2 coins can contribute to the loss of letters – in some cases making faint or weak edge lettering even harder or near impossible to see.

The image above right shows an edge inscription before and after striking. Note the difference in letter impression depth and clarity after the edge has been forced against a milled collar.

3: Manipulated / damaged after leaving The Royal Mint

Double headed coins or flipped inner section, the current minting process means that:

Any double heads or double tails you see on a UK decimal coin is almost certainly a manufactured trick coin.

Any flipped inner section of a two metal coin will have been made to deceive after the coin left The Royal Mint.

Made to deceive: flipped inner section £1 coin;
Natural environmental damage: worn and pitted metal.

Most damaged coins stand out like a sore thumb and are not errors – the metal of any coin can be changed with tools and various substances.

Always be wary of any coin that is far from the right colour (variation of colour is normal) or part of the coin is not there or the design detail is not clearly visible. Whilst there are genuine errors that would change the appearance of coins in these ways – it is also quite easy to create fake error coins like this.

Natural damage can also occur, coins left in soil or water for long periods will discolour or even blister as rust forms in the metal core of a coin with an outer layer made of another metal.

4: Fake, not produced by The Royal Mint

There are many fake coins being held in collections today, where the owner has kept it because it is not like the normal coin.

If it looks a bit wrong in a number of ways – it could be a fake. Counterfeit coins usually have poor definition in the design, (which can be seen on a phone camera when zooming in) and in bi-metal coins the gold colour may be different to what is normally seen.

If you find a £2 coin with no edge inscription, where the edge is just milled (lines) – it is almost certainly a fake.

Example: The 2011 Technology £2 coin has been faked with the Queen's portrait upside down. What initially looks like a 180 degree rotation error is just a fake coin.

If your coin falls into any of the four categories described on these pages, it is not an error coin. The following pages show images and information about UK coins that are genuine Royal Mint made errors.

UK Error Coin Types

Images and descriptions of types or categories of error that occur on UK coins struck by The Royal Mint.

The error type title is shown at the top of each page along with one or two example images.

A score is assigned based on Severity, Rarity and Desirability, this ranks the error types from 1 to 28, they are shown in rank order.

Please note that the value range shown can be wide if there are a number of variations within the error type, such as those caused by progression* or if different levels of severity could be seen.

*Progression Errors

Some coin errors begin as a small failure, which usually becomes worse as more coins are struck if the issue is not spotted and rectified.

Die Break / Cud: A broken die will continue to break under the stress of continued striking, this results in larger cuds on later struck coins.

Die Rotation Error: If a die has worked loose and begun to rotate, it is likely that it will rotate further due to machine vibrations as more coins are struck.

Collar Error (Rotation of Collar): If the collar of a non round coin works loose and begins to rotate, like die rotation, it could rotate further due to machine vibrations as more coins are struck.

Die Clash: Normally the resulting coins of a Die Clash will look similar, but there is potential for dies to clash again, deepening the existing impression.

Double Struck / Multi Struck

2010 Florence Nightingale £2 Coin; Multistruck with second and subsequent strike(s) 70% off centre.
(Image: NGC)

UK Error Type Rank: 1

Severity
Rarity
Desirability

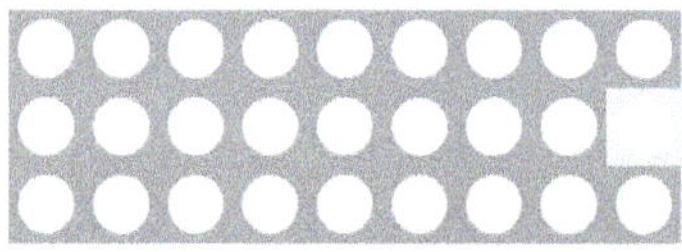

SRD Score: 26 / 30

Error coins struck more than once, range from minor to extreme with everything else in-between.

There can be a number of reasons why a coin is struck again, but at least one strike must be misaligned for the mistake in minting to be seen on the coin.

The most likely cause would be the failure of a struck coin to fully eject – it may also be possible that the timing of the strike and the circular dial plate feed mechanism become out of sync.

Associated Errors (will also be seen): Struck Off-Centre

Value Range: £20 - £350

The majority of Multi Struck coins would fall into this value range, but the 2 pound coins shown are exceptional examples that would sell above the "normal value range" for this error type.

Just looking at the few examples here, you can see why the value range for this error type is so wide, in most cases, coins looking most like normal strikes would be at the lower end of the range.

Examples that look very different, but are still clearly identifiable as a coin or specific design, will have a greater appeal to a wider market.

Error Type Examples:

Double Struck; 2018 Paddington at the Palace

Nations of the Crown £1 Coins; Double Struck

2009 Charles Darwin £2 Coin; Double Struck

Britannia 50p Coins: 1969 Double Struck and Triple Struck

Image Credits: 2006 £2 Coin; Darren, Britannia 50ps; NGC

Brockage

2010 Technology £2 Coin; Brockage. (Image: OZ)

UK Error Type Rank: 2

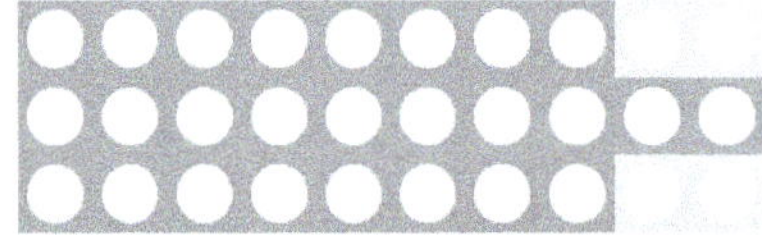

Severity
Rarity
Desirability

SRD Score: 26 / 30

In modern minting at The Royal Mint, a Brockage error is a very rare occurrence.

You will notice that the 2010 Technology £2 coin in the main image shows the normal reverse on one side and a mirror image of the same design on the other.

This happens when an already minted coin sticks to the die and strikes the next and potentially subsequent blanks with an incuse mirror image. Note that the raised design detail of the coin stuck to the die strikes an indented image.

A full brockage covers the entire face of a coin, as you would expect, a partial brockage covers only part.

Associated Errors: Die Cap

A Die Cap error is the coin that stuck to the die to create Brockage coins. This error type is not covered in this publication.

Value Range: £350 - £2000

Due to the rarity of modern UK brockage errors, setting a meaningful value range is very difficult. This error like many of the more extreme are valued on the day of sale.

Demand will be high for such an error, but a full brockage example of a popular coin design in good condition would be even more desirable.

Struck Off-Centre

Also known as: Misaligned Strike

2006 Brunel Portrait £2 coin; Struck off centre.
(Image: Frank)

UK Error Type Rank: 3

Severity
Rarity
Desirability

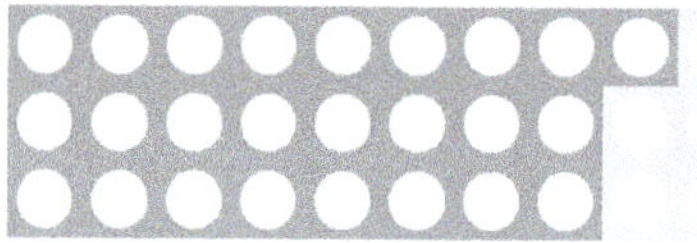

SRD Score: 25 / 30

The die and the blank were not in perfect alignment at the time of the strike. It may be that the die was misaligned or that the blank was not positioned correctly.

In the UK, The Royal Mint coin presses use a rotating disc called a dial plate to move coins into position for the strike.

If the timing of the strike and the dial plate rotation are out of sync, the strike could occur as the disc is still rotating into or out of position.

Associated Errors (may also be seen): Double Struck / Multi Struck

Value Range: £15 - £300

Demand and value depend on how far off centre the coin has been struck, 40 to 60% off are often the coins that attract the most interest.

Coins only a small amount off-centre will look too similar to the intended result, whereas some way-off strikes show very little of the coin design and may look similar to an un-struck blank.

Coins with full year dates showing on the struck part of the coin, may attract more interest than those where the date is "off the edge".

Error Type Examples:

Slight Off Centre Strike

Double Struck, Second Strike Off Centre (Image: NGC)

A more extreme Off Centre Strike (Image: NGC)
2015 First World War Navy £2 Coin

60% Off Centre Strike (Image: OZ)

Nations of the Crown £1: 2017 Struck 35% Off Centre and 2016 Struck Off Centre with Straight Clip shown below.

A number of Struck Off Centre coins also have clips present - it is possible that the incomplete blank makes an incorrect position for striking more likely.

Struck on Un-punched Planchet

Also known as: Mono-Metallic, Single Metal

2015 Britannia £2 Coin; Struck on Un-punched nickel-brass blank. (Image: The Royal Mint Museum)

UK Error Type Rank: 4

Severity
Rarity
Desirability

SRD Score: 24 / 30

A blank missed the hole punch process due to machine failure or a blank storage and distribution issue.

The hole punch is one of the last steps in bi-metal blank production, this error could be caused by a machine feed issue, but it is thought the most common cause is when a blank simply misses the hole punch process, ending up with the holed blanks ready to be struck.

It may also be possible for two blanks to enter the punch at the same time and the punch fails to hole one or both. It is known that this can occur in striking: see "Two Planchets Struck Together".

This error can be seen on bi-metal coins, UK £1 and £2 coins struck by The Royal Mint for circulation and coins struck as Brilliant Uncirculated.

Value Range: £300 - £1200

There are a number of variations within this error type, hence the wide value range.

At auction, an un-punched planchet commemorative £2 coin would be expected to realise a higher price than definitive £1 and £2 coins struck in multiple years.

Error Type Examples:

Definitive Nations of the Crown £1 and Technology £2
Struck on Un-punched Planchets

Commemorative £2 coins struck on un-punched nickel-brass blanks; 2010 Florence Nightingale, 2014 First World War Centenary (Images: The Royal Mint Museum) and 2015 First World War Navy (Image: Anton).

Struck Through

Also known as: Struck Thru, Strike Thru

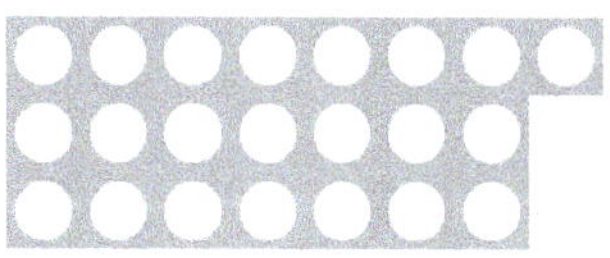

1978 Britannia 50p; Obverse struck through a previously
struck metal fragment. (Image: NGC)

UK Error Type Rank: 5

Severity
Rarity
Desirability

SRD Score: 22 / 30

If any object that should not be there comes between the
die and blank as struck, the resulting Struck Through coin
will show some evidence of the object that got in the way.

If only an impression of the object is visible on the coin, it may be possible to determine what was there. If the object or part of it is embedded in the coin, the error would be referred to as Struck Through Retained.

Small fragments of metal are the most common items that are struck through in modern minting.

Value Range: £10 - £300

Most struck through coins would fall into this value range, the effect the item had on the coin and whether it was retained will dictate demand and final selling price. The 50p in the main image is an exceptional example that would sell above the "normal value range" for this error type.

Error Type Examples:

Reverse Struck Through, Retained Brass (Image: NGC)

Most coins of this error type will only show evidence of the struck through item on one side, as in this case where the obverse looks normal.

Obverse Struck Through Capped Die

Obverse Struck Through

Overstruck (Existing coin, not blank)

Also known as: Overstrike

2013 20p; Overstruck on 2012 Trinidad 25c. (Image: NGC)

UK Error Type Rank: 6

Severity
Rarity
Desirability

SRD Score: 21 / 30

An already struck coin, UK or foreign, ended up with blanks to be struck for UK coins.

The resulting Overstruck coin will show strong design elements of the most recent strike, with underlying fainter elements of the coin design of the first strike.

Associated Errors (very likely to also be seen): Foreign "Planchet" / Coin or Wrong Denomination "Planchet" / Coin

Value Range: £60 - £300

The visual effect (and in turn value) is dependent on which coin is struck for which UK design and how much / which parts of the original coin design are still visible.

Nations of the Crown £1 Overstruck on Struck and hole punched 2016 Shield 20p

Image: The Royal Mint Museum

An unlikely mixed denomination given that a struck 20p is only slightly bigger than the £1 inner blank.

A 2016 20p was hole punched with £1 outer blanks and received an inner pill which is of course thicker than a 20p, the strike mostly hit the inner pill leaving the remaining 20p design near complete.

This coin did not leave the factory and is part of a collection held with The Royal Mint Museum.

Obverse: Nations of the Crown £1 Overstruck on Struck
and hole punched 2016 Shield 20p
(Image: The Royal Mint Museum)

You can just about make out the 12 sides on the 20p outer,
as the expansion of the inner pill just about pushed the 20p
to the £1 collar.

Error Type Examples:

20p Overstruck on Struck 2009 1p 3.5g

2p Overstruck on Struck Egypt 1 Pound (Image: NGC)

This coin does look like and technically is a Foreign Planchet error - but if you look closely, very feint design details of the overstruck coin can be seen below "TWO PENCE" and on the right side.

Broadstrike

Also known as: Broadstruck

2004 1p; Broadstruck. (Image: The Royal Mint Museum)

UK Error Type Rank: 7

Severity
Rarity
Desirability

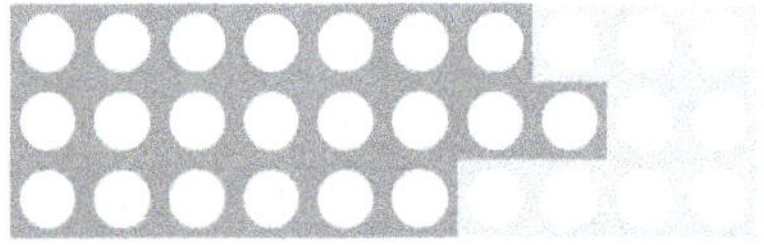

SRD Score: 21 / 30

There are a few different looking errors classed as Broadstrike. The classic interpretation would be a coin struck without a collar (or perhaps also outside of the collar), where in a normal strike, the collar surrounds the blank to stop metal flowing outward when struck to create a coin with a clean edge.

A strike without a collar present would create a flatter and wider coin than normal.

If you see a coin like this in change or whilst hunting though coin bags, it is a great find that nobody could miss.

So if this is a broadstruck coin, why do we see coins looking completely different also labelled as broadstruck?

It seems that any issue with the collar can end up with a broadstruck label, if the collar is in place but mis-aligned / rotated, metal flow will be mostly retained within the collar.

In this book, we will stick with the classic interpretation, any error where the collar is not missing will be in the Collar Error category, which includes Partial Collar Errors.

Value Range: £25 - £160

Error Type Examples:

2010 Technology £2 Coin; Broadstruck

1971 1p; Broadstruck. (Image: OZ)

2009 Kew Gardens 50p; Broadstruck

Wrong Denomination Planchet

Also known as: Struck on 1p Planchet (etc)

50p Struck on 1p Blank. (Image: NGC)

UK Error Type Rank: 8

Severity
Rarity
Desirability

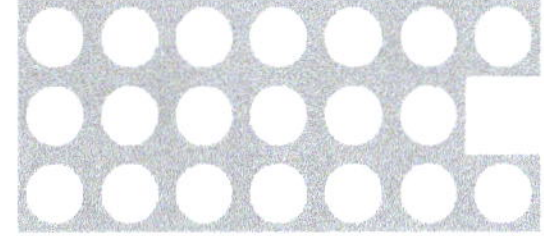

SRD Score: 20 / 30

A blank intended for a different UK denomination ended up with 1p, 2p, 5p, 10p, 20p, 50p, £1, £2 or even Crown / £5 blanks.

A fascinating error category with many possibilities, eight circulating denomination blanks could end up being struck as who knows what – I am sure there are a number of impossible or very unlikely combinations based on blank sizes and the current minting process.

Value Range: £25 - £1000

Wrong Planchet errors can be so varied that a guide value range based on this error type isn't particularly helpful.

Error coin collectors are looking for the different and perhaps even extreme, so a 20p struck on a 5p blank, looks quite like a 20p (See Error Type Examples). The similar looking coins like this would be valued towards the lower end of the range.

The main image shows a 1p coin blank struck as a 50p – everything is different, a shape and colour we don't expect to see. An error such as this would attract more interest.

An unlikely denomination swap was seen in 1981, when a 50p blank was struck as a 25p crown.

1981 Royal Wedding Crown; Struck on a 50p Planchet.

This coin was added to the Coin Hunter error coin database in 2023, it had been in the hands of the owner for over 40 years.

In 1981, Royal Wedding Commemorative Crowns were being placed in packaging, this coin was at the bottom of a box of crowns - upon showing the find, the worker was told to keep it as a souvenir.

Sadly, all that remains today are these images and an authentication letter from The Royal Mint Museum. It disappeared in the post on the return journey from authentication. Royal Mail paid just £350 in compensation despite being informed by The Royal Mint Museum that it was a genuine rare coin, having not come across another like it in the last decade.

Error Type Examples:

50p Struck on 5p Planchet 3.2g

2p Struck on 1p Planchet 3.6g

2p Struck on 10p Planchet
(Image: The Royal Mint Museum)

20p Struck on 5p Planchet 3.25g

1988 5p Struck On 1p Planchet (Image: OZ)

1971 2p Struck On 5p Planchet (Image: OZ)

Mule

Mixed Denomination Mule: 2001 Marconi Wireless
Transmission £2 / 2p Coin

UK Error Type Rank: 9

Severity
Rarity
Desirability

SRD Score: 20 / 30

A coin referred to as a mule error occurs when mismatched dies are installed in a coin press, the blank is struck with reverse and obverse designs that should not be together on the same coin. This can result in coins without any date / denomination.

This error name is a reference to something that should not be, likened to the offspring of a donkey and a horse which is called a "Mule".

Value Range: £50 - £1600

Current values for 4 of the 6 coins described on the following pages are shown on the "The 10 Most Publicised UK Coin Errors" page.

Ranging from a guide price of £50 for the Undated 20p to over £1000 for the 2009 Crowned Lion Passant 10p and the No Denomination 2014 First World War £2 Coin. In 2015 a 2009 Crowned Lion Passant 10p sold for £750, very few examples are known, another did sell more recently for £1600.

The coin in the main image made with a 2001 £2 reverse die and a 2001 2p obverse die is likely unique and would exceed the top end value which applies to most UK mule errors.

To be the first to identify a previously unknown mule, you would need to know exactly what the obverse side of each coin should look like.

If a machine had been set up with mis-matched dies, it would be expected that the production run would be large enough to ensure this type of error on a specific coin would be identified shortly after entering circulation.

These are the three circulation coins you should be checking, to see if you can find the mule version.

Undated 20p

In November 2008 a number of 20p coins (less than 250,000) were struck with a new tails and old heads die. An undated mule coin was the result of this error, as neither die included the 2008 date.

No Denomination 2014 First World War £2 Coin

The use of the Trinity House £2 heads die on this design means that the mule created does not show a denomination of TWO POUNDS.

At the time of writing, it is surprising how few of the "No Denomination 2014 First World War £2 Coin" have been found - this is not what would be expected if any sort of normal production run occurred with the incorrect obverse die.

This could not be investigated further as The Royal Mint do not have any production information from 2014 or earlier, as the information has been disposed of in line with their data retention policies.

Duel Dated 2016 Nations of the Crown £1 Coin

A tails die showing the date 2017 in micro-lettering was paired with a heads die dated 2016.

There were also 2 mules created in Brilliant Uncirculated quality for Royal Mint sets. These would be very unlikely to turn up in change or bank bags.

1983 NEW PENCE 2p

In 1982 the 2p inscription was changed to TWO PENCE but a small number of 1983-dated 2p coins were struck in error bearing the old NEW PENCE inscription.

2009 Crowned Lion Passant 10p

In 2008 the 10p coin design changed from the Crowned Lion Passant to the Shield design by Matthew Dent. A very small number of 2009 dated 10p coins were struck in error using the old Crowned Lion Passant reverse die.

Defective Planchet

2008 Shield 10p; Struck on Defective Planchet (4.8g); a normal 10p weighs about 6.5 grams. (Image: NGC)

UK Error Type Rank: 10

SRD Score: 20 / 30

Defective Panchet - defects due to issues in production and rolling out the metal, rather than those created by a punching error.

As the coin metal is rolled out, tensile stresses can tear open the strip, leaving holes and fissures. This can occur if the strip is brittle due to the presence of contaminants or because it wasn't heated to a high enough temperature prior to rolling.

Associated Errors: Lamination

Value Range: £10 - £200

Defective Planchet (Image: The Royal Mint Museum)

Defective Planchet (Image: The Royal Mint Museum)

Struck on Defective Planchet 7.2g

Struck on Defective Planchet 4.2g

Struck on Defective Planchet 2.5g

Struck on Defective Planchet 7g

A normal 50p would weigh about 8 grams, the blank struck for this coin was missing 1 gram of metal.

Withdrawn Version

2011 Aquatics 50p / London 2012 sports collection pack; Withdrawn Version. (Image: NGC)

UK Error Type Rank: 11

Severity	
Rarity	
Desirability	

SRD Score: 20 / 30

If a coin is struck with a design that is superseded by a new version, the original dies would no longer be used.

If the coin stocks are still on site, the struck coins would most likely be recycled. If any of the coins left the site, a variation of the intended design will exist, as it would not be possible to recall such coins.

These are not error coins, as no recognised error is present, they are however evidence of some sort of error or mistake in design or production timing.

At this time there are only two decimal coins produced by The Royal Mint that fit this category. The 2011 Aquatics 50p original version with lines over the swimmers face and the 2019 Withdrawal from the EU (Brexit) 50p.

Note: 2019, not 2020 for the Brexit 50p – as coins were struck dated 2019 showing one of the Brexit dates that didn't happen, 31 October 2019, on the reverse.

This coin is not an urban myth, one or some did leave the factory by means unknown.

This poor quality image is captured from a video that showed both sides of a genuine 2019 dated coin.

Realistically it's not worth checking your change for these two coins, one was sold in collector packs only in small numbers and the other probably exists in numbers similar to the 1933 Penny or less.

Value Range: £2500+

It's very hard these days to find a **genuine*** 2011 Aquatics (in pack) original design version for less than £2,500.

*There are now quite a few different fake versions of this coin, real circulated Aquatics 50ps are also defaced to add lines on the swimmers face. Our advice: If looking to buy, deal with a Specialist Numismatic Auction House or a Coin Dealer who is a member of the BNTA (British Numismatic Trade Association).

The "near myth" 2019 Brexit 50p dated 31 October 2019 would be worth what someone would pay for it – but there are questions about how a marked for destruction (or recycling) coin still exists.

Struck on Inner or Outer Only

Also known as: Struck on Centre Insert, Missing Centre Insert

2002 Commonwealth Games England £2 Coin; Struck on Centre Insert (6g). (Image: NGC)

UK Error Type Rank: 12

Severity
Rarity
Desirability

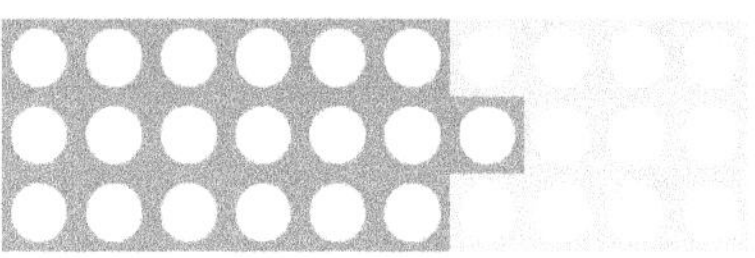

SRD Score: 19 / 30

Bi-metal coins struck by The Royal Mint for circulation are made up of 2 blanks that are fed in one after the other.

The outer with the hole punched out is fed in first and the inner "pill" is then fed into the hole. When struck the pressure connects the 2 parts into a bi-metal coin that requires a great deal of force to break apart.

If the feed fails to deliver an outer, the dies will strike just the inner.

If the feed fails to deliver an inner pill into the hole, the dies will strike just the outer.

Associated Errors: Offset Centre Insert: If the inner fails to seat correctly in the hole, an Offset Centre Insert error will result from the strike. Sometimes the insert does not remain attached, errors described as "Missing Centre Insert" should show evidence that the other part was present when struck.

Value Range: £30 - £200

Coins struck on the inner pill of a £1 coin will be at the lower end of the guide value range. £2 coins, especially commemorative designs should achieve closer to the high end of the range.

2019 £1 Struck Without Centre Insert

Struck on Centre Insert 3.8g

2018 £1 Double Struck Without Centre Insert (Image: OZ)

Offset Centre Insert

Also known as: Fried Egg Error

2014 First World War Centenary £2; Offset Centre Insert.

UK Error Type Rank: 13

Severity	
Rarity	
Desirability	

SRD Score: 18 / 30

The silver inner pill (blank) was not fully seated within the outer ring when struck.

The inner blank not centred is fairly common in production of the new 12 sided bi-metallic £1 coin, it is seen much less often on the larger, round £2 coins.

If the silver pill is not fully within the hole in the outer ring, the strike will produce what is affectionately known in the UK as a fried egg error, where the silver "yolk" spills out into the gold. (There will also be some gold design elements that should be part of the silver inner on the opposing side of the coin)

This error can be initiated at the hole punch stage, if the outer blank is pierced at a slight angle instead of straight, a lip exists than can stop the inner blank dropping fully into position.

The error has been seen for both UK bi-metal denominations struck by The Royal Mint for circulation and coins struck as Brilliant Uncirculated.

2021 Walter Scott £2 Coin; Offset Centre Insert
Brilliant Uncirculated (Not Struck For Circulation)

Unlike coins for circulation, where the inner and outer blanks are fed in separately just before striking, the process for Brilliant Uncirculated coins would normally see the 2 parts "pre-assembled" to create a bi-metal blank ready to strike.

If this is the normal process at The Royal Mint, Offset Centre Insert errors on Brilliant Uncirculated coins should be much less likely.

Associated Errors: When the centre pill is not in the correct position, the strike is often unbalanced causing a **Partial Collar Error** in the position where the inner pill metal has spread outwards, pushing the outer metal over the top of the collar.

If the offset is large the centre insert may not be retained after the strike, see Missing Centre Insert in the previous section. In this case the parts remained together but were not securely connected.

2013 Golden Guinea £2 Coin; Offset Centre Insert

Value Range: £40 - £200

There are varying degrees of severity within this error type, hence the wide value range. The easily visible silver and gold overspill of metals makes this an appealing and desirable error.

The amount of overspill, coin design / denomination, as well as the design elements affected will be factors impacting demand and price.

Error Type Examples:

2017, 2019 and 2020 Nations of the Crown £1 Coins; Offset Centre Insert

2012 Charles Dickens £2 Coin; Offset Centre Insert

2016 First World War Army £2 Coin; Offset Centre Insert

In the example above, the effect is only really seen on the obverse of the coin - so take a good look at both sides if you're hunting for this type of error in change or bank bags.

Foreign Planchet

Also known as: Off-Metal Strike

2009 Shield 2p; Overstruck on Struck Egypt 1 Pound (8.5g). (Image: NGC)

UK Error Type Rank: 14

Severity
Rarity
Desirability

SRD Score: 18 / 30

A blank intended for a foreign coin where the country orders either coins or blanks from The Royal Mint, ended up with blanks to be struck for UK coins.

The visual effect is dependent on which foreign blank is struck for which UK denomination - some result in coins looking similar to a normal coin and some are much more interesting and appealing.

This 2021 HG Wells £2 is an exceptional example, struck with the correct outer and foreign blank inner. The incorrect inner made of steel was much smaller than the correct cupro-nickel inner.

As a result the outer ring expanded to fill the space and create a thinner, lighter coin with more of the design in the gold coloured outer.

All error type value ranges in this book relate to the majority of coins of a specific type, there will always be exceptional examples that would sell for more than the high end of the range. This HG Wells £2 sold for over £1000, as this type of error is rarely seen on bi-metal coins.

Value Range: £20 - £250

Foreign Planchet errors can create many different variations – coins that look just like expected in terms of colour, size and shape will be at the lower end of the value range – whereas off-metal strikes that are the wrong colour or shape will attract higher bids.

Error Type Examples:

Struck on Foreign Planchets: 2013 Christopher Ironside
50p, 2011 1p (Images: The Royal Mint Museum)

2p Struck on Foreign Planchet 2.5g (Image: NGC)

2004 10p Struck on Foreign Holed Planchet
(Image: The Royal Mint Museum)

1990 20p Struck on Foreign Planchet 2.6g

2011 20p Struck on Foreign Planchet 2.8g

2011 Tennis 50p Struck on Foreign Blank 2.9g

1997 50p Struck on Foreign Scalloped Planchet 6g

2005 Gunpowder Plot £2 Struck on Foreign Blank 10.4g

Two Planchets Struck Together

Also known as: Uni-face Coin

20p Reverse Half of Two Planchets Struck Together.
(Image: NGC)

UK Error Type Rank: 15

Severity
Rarity
Desirability

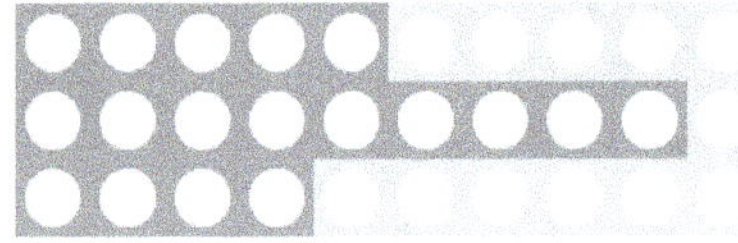

SRD Score: 18 / 30

Two blanks stuck together or fed in together are struck between the dies, creating a pair of single sided coins.

As the two blanks stacked on top of each other are struck a matched pair is produced, one with only an obverse image, and a second with only the reverse image.

It would be very unlikely that the pair will remain together and be found together – both coins will look normal from one side and like a blank from the other.

A coin with one blank side is very easy to spot, so would likely be removed from circulation by the first person to notice the error.

To be in with a chance of finding this error, you would need to get hold of new sealed bags as new coins are being released into circulation for the first time.

Value Range: £40 - £120

A reverse or obverse that can be connected to a specific year dated coin can sometimes help push the value up.

A marked increase in interest and value would be expected if both the reverse and obverse from a matched pair are together.

Clipped Planchet

Also known as: Clip, Clips, Clipped Flan

2016 Shakespeare Histories £2; Triple Curved Clips on Inner Planchet.

UK Error Type Rank: 16

Severity
Rarity
Desirability

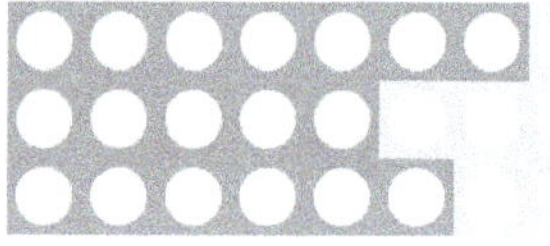

SRD Score: 18 / 30

Planchets or Blanks are punched from a strip of metal by a blanking press. If there is an issue with the feed through the machine, blanks can be punched from incomplete parts of the sheet.

If the punch overlaps existing holes, blanks with one or more sections missing will be produced, a curved part circle for round blanks or a part equilateral curve heptagon for 50ps.

Note: 50p blanks are punched as equilateral curve heptagons, 20p blanks are round.

If the punch overlaps the edge of the sheet, a blank with a straight edged section missing can be punched or a ragged clip can occur if the unfinished metal at the end of a roll is punched.

So the clip or clips are already there when the blank is struck, this makes a genuine clipped coin look different to one that has been cut after striking to resemble an error.

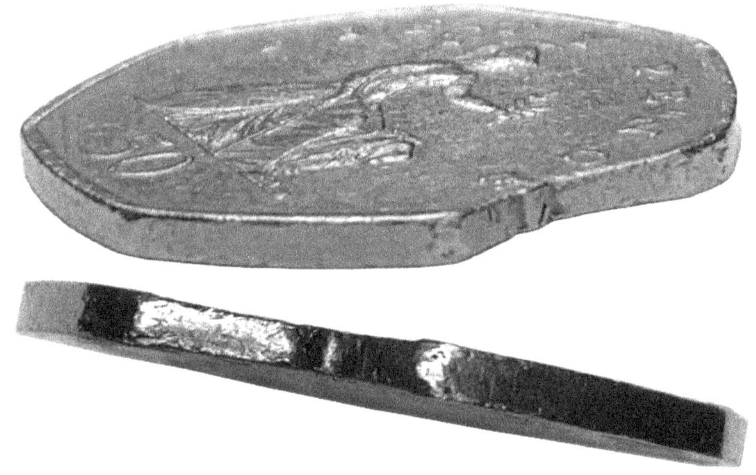

The image above shows a genuine clip, note the concave appearance of the metal edge.

Clipped Planchet errors are one of the most often faked coin errors in the UK, as it is easy to cut bits off coins. Our advice: If looking to buy, only deal with a company or person you trust. Always inspect the edge closely.

Finding "Clipped Planchet" errors:

This error can affect any denomination, anything other than a very small clip will be obvious as you take a first look at the coin – to ensure you don't miss any, it can help to hold a number of coins in the palm of your hand like a coin roll and then tilt your hand to check all edges line up.

When checking bi-metal coins, the outer or the inner blank can be clipped – look for a hole between the silver and gold parts of the coin to spot an inner blank clip.

Value Range: £5 - £180

Error coins with multiple clips are rarer and can be more valuable than a single clip coin. Inner blank clips on £2 coins are quite interesting so could attract higher bids.

Error Type Examples:

2019 Sherlock Holmes 50p; Double Curved Clips

2005 20p; Clip (Image: The Royal Mint Museum)

2017 Nations of the Crown £1 Coin; Curved Clip on Unpunched Planchet (Image: The Royal Mint Museum)

1971 1p; Double Curved Clips

2014 Shield 10p; Triple Curved Clips

2014 Shield 50p; Double Curved Clips

2007 Abolition of the Slave Trade £2; Double Curved Clips

Die Rotation

Also known as: Rotated Dies

UK Error Type Rank: 17

Severity
Rarity
Desirability

SRD Score: 16 / 30

In the UK, the reverse and obverse dies should line up with the top of each design at the 12 o'clock position.

It is possible due to the human factor, that dies are installed with one rotated in comparison to the other, this may well be the case for rotation errors found on 50p and 20p coins. In the case of round coins, it is likely that many rotations are the result of one of the dies working loose.

It makes sense that vibrations during normal operation of the coining press could rotate a die, gradually moving towards 180 degrees of rotation if the issue is not spotted.

Small amounts of rotation are not uncommon on UK coins, especially in production of round coins.

Many collectors would be looking for at least 45 degrees, perhaps even a quarter turn (90 degrees) before taking a second look.

To check a coin for rotation, simply turn it over like the page of a book. As a denomination, £2 coins are worth checking, especially known issue coins such as:

2015 Definitive Britannia and Technology (up to 180°)
2009 Technology (up to 90°)
2007 Act of Union (up to 90°)
2002 Commonwealth Games Wales (up to 180°)
1999 Rugby World Cup (up to 180°)

2017 Benjamin Bunny 50p Rotation Error: When Benjamin is the right way up, the portrait is out of line by 1 of the 7 sides (about 50°), also check your 2006 Britannia 50ps.

2005 20p with about 15° of rotation (Image: Roger Terry)

Check your 2005 20p coins for a part side rotation, also check 2008 Shield 5p coins as some have been found with 180° of rotation.

If you find a 50p coin which looks a small amount out of line with the shape, it may be a slight die rotation if the other side looks normal. If the rotation is significant, see the "Collar Error" section which includes collar rotation errors.

Value Range: £10 - £80

When it comes to rotation errors, upside down (180 degrees or close to it) is best for round coins, anything a quarter turn or more would also attract some interest, with less demand for coins as the portrait gets closer to the normal position.

50p coins, look for the portrait being 1 side out of alignment, 2017 Benjamin Bunny 50p errors are not uncommon, but any 50p rotated by more than 1 side would attract interest. Also check 20p and £1 coins as small or 1 side rotation errors are possible.

Split Planchet

UK Error Type Rank: 18

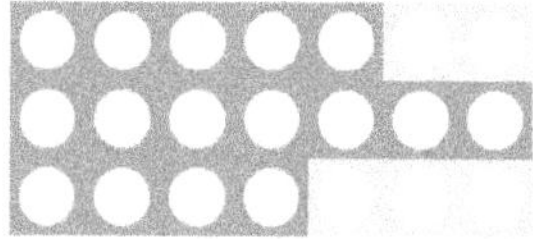

Severity
Rarity
Desirability

SRD Score: 16 / 30

In the very early stages of the minting process, metal alloys rolled into sheets may contain impurities under the surface such as gas, dirt, or grease. Blanks punched from these sheets have an underlying weakness which can result in the metal peeling and splitting apart along the edge to create two parts (full diameter but thin and light).

Split Planchet errors are very unlikely to affect modern coins produced by The Royal Mint. They are normally only seen on coins made from a solid alloy, such as 1p and 2p coins struck before September 1992.

There are two types of Split Planchet error, split before strike and split after strike. A "split before strike" will show design on both sides with one side also showing lines of ridges and furrows where the split occurred.

A thin 3.9g coin, just over half the weight of a normal 2p. Lines show on the obverse, so this will have been the "split" side of the blank. (Image: NGC)

A "split after strike" will look normal on one side, but will have a rougher surface perhaps with some unclear design showing on the other side.

If you find a 1p or 2p that feels a bit light, check if the date is 1992 or earlier (or 1998 as well for 2ps). You may have found a Split Planchet error, check the weight to be sure, a normal 1p should weight about 3.56g and a 2p 7.12g, a Split Planchet will always be a reasonable amount lighter.

Associated Errors: Lamination

Value Range: £20 - £100

A marked increase in interest and value would be expected if both parts of a "split after strike" coin are offered for sale together.

Lamination

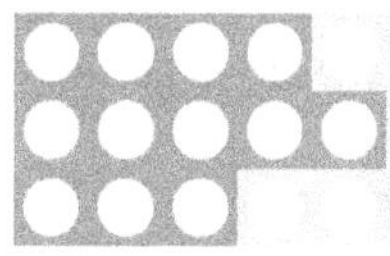

2006 50p Reverse Lamination. (Image: NGC)

UK Error Type Rank: 19

Severity
Rarity
Desirability

SRD Score: 12 / 30

In the world of numismatic errors, the term lamination is applied to any coin where the metal begins to come apart due to metal impurities present in the creation of an alloy used for blanks.

The term "lamination error" is a generic term to cover any failure in metal cohesion. Whilst alloys should not contain an specific "layers", errors of this type occur when any foreign matter compromises the structure of the blank.

The coin may show a peeling or flaking layer of metal with an appearance of metal leaf when retained or a grainy appearance where detached. Some coins of this error type may develop cracks, where metal can lift along the crack edges.

2005 50p Obverse Lamination (Image: OZ)

If the planchet splits into two on the horizontal axis (like lifting one dinner plate off another), it is known as a Split Planchet error - which is just a more extreme "lamination" error.

Associated Errors: Split Planchet

Value Range: £5 - £60

As each metal cohesion issue will create a different looking coin surface, value of this type of error will depend on what buyers like to see. A glimmering metal leaf appearance on 50% of the coin could attract more interest than a small crack with a lifting edge.

Error Type Examples:

Obverse Lamination

Reverse Lamination

Die Clash

2016 Jemima Puddle-Duck Die Clash; obverse die shown, outline of portrait on reverse.

UK Error Type Rank: 20

Severity
Rarity
Desirability

SRD Score: 11 / 30

If the blank feed system fails to deliver and site a blank between the dies, they can collide with each other, potentially damaging each die and imprinting design elements from one to the other.

The dies operate with a safety margin (minimum die clearance) so would normally not touch if there is no blank present, but these margins can change during machine operation – although very rare, if the clearance is zero or less when a blank feed fails, the dies will clash.

As with many of the coin minting processes, there is a human factor to consider, mistakes in setting up machinery could account for some die clash occurrences.

Any damage to the dies will then be visible on every subsequent blank struck until the dies are changed.

Finding "Die Clash" errors:

Check both sides the coin for outlines of design from the opposite side, the outlines can be quite faint or easily noticeable – depending on how much damage occurred as the dies collided.

This error is known to have happened to dies striking the 2016 Jemima Puddle-Duck 50p and 2017 Sir Isaac Newton 50p.

The orbit lines showing on the obverse is quite common on the 2017 Sir Isaac Newton 50p. (Image: Roger Terry)

Other 50p die clashes to look out for in change include the 1998 NHS 50p, a number of the 2011 Olympic Sports designs (Basketball, Football, Pentathlon, Shooting and Wheelchair Rugby), 2015 Battle of Britain, 2017 Peter Rabbit and 2018 Representation of the People Act.

Value Range: £5 - £35

Value will depend on the coin design and how clearly the outlines can be seen on the reverse / obverse or both. The 2016 Jemima Puddle-Duck 50p is a popular coin and strong Die Clash imprints have been seen on some examples.

Wrong Edge Inscription

UK Error Type Rank: 21

Severity
Rarity
Desirability

SRD Score: 11 / 30

The edge inscription is added to the blank before the coin is struck. This error occurs when blanks intended for use with a specific £2 coin design, end up in the hopper of a machine fitted with dies for a different £2 coin.

Where larger numbers of this error are found, such as the 2016 Shakespeare Tragedies £2 coin struck onto blanks intended for the 2016 First World War Army £2 coin, it is very likely that a part filled box of "FOR KING AND COUNTRY" edge lettered blanks (estimate: 15,000) were tipped into a machine set up with Shakespeare Tragedies dies.

Where lower numbers of mismatched edge lettering coins are discovered, it is likely that some blanks remained in a hopper where dies were subsequently changed or a few remained in a box after tipping into a hopper, with the box then filled with blanks for a different coin.

Check the edge of any Shakespeare Tragedies £2 you find in change, as the error coin reading "FOR KING AND COUNTRY" entered circulation in quite large numbers.

Two other £2 coins worth checking:

2006 Brunel Portrait, a few coins have been found with the edge inscription from the 2005 Gunpowder Plot £2 "REMEMBER REMEMBER FIFTH OF NOVEMBER".

2016 First World War Army with the inscription from the Great Fire of London £2 "THE WHOLE CITY IN DREADFUL FLAMES".

Value Range: £20 - £60

Whilst interesting, most edge inscription errors don't reach high values.

Coins where the error is well known and relatively common, sell for about £25. Others where the mistake has involved far fewer blanks are not often offered for sale, but should achieve more than the Shakespeare Tragedies edge inscription error.

Die Break / Cud

Also known as: Die Crack / Die Chip

UK Error Type Rank: 22

Severity
Rarity
Desirability

SRD Score: 10 / 30

The dies are continuously striking metal blanks at a rate of about 12 per second, this places significant load on the dies, wear and tear will eventually result in damage.

Any cracks or missing bits of the die fill with metal as the blank is struck, producing a raised metal line or blob known as a cud.

There is of course a cost involved in making dies from hardened steel, so whilst most dies should remain in good condition for 250,000 strikes, there are a few reasons why we will see blobs of metal on many current and future coins.

A die could be used for more strikes than a recommended limit, or it could simply fail earlier than anticipated.

Whatever the reason, as soon as bits start falling off a die, things will only get worse – every coin struck from that moment until the die is replaced, will have metal where it was not supposed to be.

The most famous and possibly most common UK cud error began as a very small crack in the reverse die for the 2015 First World War Navy £2.

The crack happened to be on a horizontal section at the top of the mast. Coins struck as the crack first formed are known as the "sleeping cat error" presumably in reference to a ship's cat.

As the crack grew and small bits of the die broke away, it began to form a shape that very much resembled a flag flying on the mast.

The left image shows a Partial Flag or "Sleeping Cat" error, a Full Flag error is shown on the right.

Whilst any coin could be found with raised blobs of metal as a result of die damage, it is always worth checking your 2015 First World War Navy £2 coins for the flag error.

Some designs and coins are more susceptible to die break errors, take a look at all Shield 10ps, especially around the lion's legs and feet near the edge of the coin.

This type of error can be sub classed based on the expected cause of the error, overused dies that are failing may produce coins labeled as Die "Deterioration" rather than "Break" - where perhaps a cleaner, crisper look to the error may be observed. The heads side of 20ps seem to show signs of die deterioration more than other coins, the 2012 20p is one example.

This coin is part of The Royal Mint Museum's error coin collection, a similar 20p was found in the book research coin hunt, see the "20p Coin Hunting" section.

Value Range: £2 - £25

Not any great value in this type of error in most cases, with the famous Navy £2 cat / part flag / full flag errors selling for £5 to £10.

Coins where the cud is larger, it looks like something or blobs are in an interesting position are more likely to reach the higher values.

Collar Error

Royal Arms Shield £1 Coin; Collar Error, 7 sided collar
(Image: The Royal Mint Museum)

UK Error Type Rank: 23

Severity
Rarity
Desirability

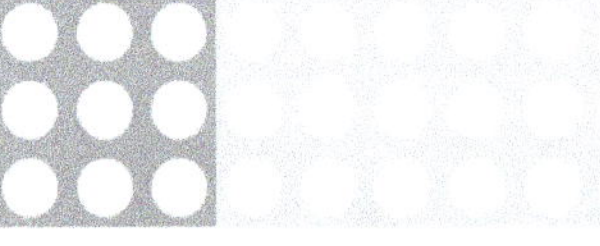

SRD Score: 9 / 30

The collar surrounds the blank at the point it is struck, this keeps the metal contained to create a uniform edge that is usually plain like a 50p or milled (vertical lines) like a £2 coin.

In this publication we have separated the three errors related to the collar as:

Broadstrike: No collar in place or struck outside of the collar. (See separate Broadstrike Error section)

Collar Error: Incorrect collar or other issue with the collar in place, such as mis-aligned or damaged.

The collar is what adds the milled edge to coins such as the ten pence piece, on a few occasions, notably in 2016 a 10p press was fitted with a plain edge collar instead of the correct milled edge collar.

A coin with the milled edge missing would fall into this category, as would 50ps where the collar has rotated – although others have classified these as broadstruck.

The collar that holds the blank/coin has rotated to no longer match the alignment of the dies.

2010 Girlguiding 50p; Collar Rotation Error

If the design position does not match the 50p shape, it will either be a slight die rotation if just 1 side is out of line, or a Collar Rotation Error, if both sides are out of line, but line up with each other when the coin is turned like a page in a book. (As shown in the image above)

Partial Collar Error: The correct collar is complete and in the right position, but the blank did not position properly within the collar before being struck, as the result the metal was only partially contained by the collar.

A variety of £1 coin Partial Collar errors

One part of the edge shows contact with the collar whilst the other displays features consistent with it being outside of the collar – such as a lip of metal extending past the normal edge of the coin or a part smooth edge that should have been milled.

Collar Errors can occur in striking any UK coin denomination, but Partial Collar Errors are more common on non-round coins such as the 12 sided £1, bi-metal creates even more potential for issues during the minting process.

This is an error that can be found in your change: for the reasons mentioned above, it is most often seen on the £1 coin, look for a "lip of metal" on the edge of the coin.

Associated Errors: Many of the **Offset Centre Insert** error £1 coins also exhibit a Partial Collar Error, this is because the offset centre pill increases the amount a metal flowing to one side of the collar.

Value Range: £2 - £20

The coin in the main image, a 7 sided £1 coin is an exceptional collar error that would be very unlikely to reach the public. This coin is an example from the error collection held by The Royal Mint Museum. This collection is made up of errors that were spotted before they could end up in circulation.

The majority of normal collar errors would fall within the value range, but if a mixed denomination wrong collar coin was ever offered for sale, it would sell for significantly more.

Error Type Example:

2011 Triathlon 50p; Collar Rotation Error

Planchet Plating

2008 10p Partial Wrong Plating
(Image: The Royal Mint Museum)

UK Error Type Rank: 24

Severity
Rarity
Desirability

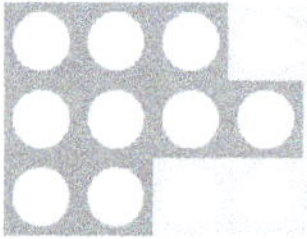

SRD Score: 9 / 30

A blank missed the plating process or was not correctly plated.

In the UK this error could be seen on any coin where blanks are plated with another metal, such as 1p and 2p coins which are made of Copper-plated steel (since September 1992), 5p and 10p coins which are made of Nickel-plated steel (since January 2012) and the 12 sided £1 coin inner which is made from Nickel plated brass.

Steel is magnetic, so you can check what these UK coins are made of using a magnet. 2011 10ps are magnetic, so were likely struck in early 2012 with a 2011 date.

A planchet plating error will likely be a different colour than a correctly plated coin, but be wary, as the appearance of any plated coin can be easily altered.

When looking at any coin where the colour of the metal is not what is expected, consider all the possibilities, as just as plating can be chemically removed after the coin is struck, another layer of plating could also be applied.

Coins that have missed the plating process would look very similar to coins that have been manipulated to deceive.

Value Range: £5 - £40

2014 1p Partially Plated Planchet

2006 1p Improperly Annealed

This coin example is included in this category, even though the plating is complete, during the process of heating the blanks (Annealing) - plating discolouration can occur.

Doubling (Die or Strike)

Also known as: Doubled Die / Doubled Image

2010 Technology £2; Die Doubling (Image: Roger Terry)

UK Error Type Rank: 25

Severity
Rarity
Desirability

SRD Score: 8 / 30

Doubling as the name suggests is where design details on a coin appear twice, often seen most clearly on lettering, it can look like an original and shadow.

It can be caused by a slight movement of a die as it connects with the blank (Strike Doubling) or by a die manufacture fault called hub doubling when a master die is created. (Die Doubling)

A Master Die for the 2010 Technology £2 Coin was created with doubled details on the obverse, when checking 2010 Technology £2 coins, take a close look at the letters in ELIZABETH – as this is where the Doubling can be seen clearest.

Double struck coins where the strikes were a few millimetres apart would also show doubled design details – but the effect of two separate strikes would be much starker than a single strike die movement.

Value Range: £5 - £40

Die fatigue, where the die is worn (perhaps through overuse) can create a similar "doubled" look to the text and images.

One example of an overused die can be seen here, in 2013 the obverse die used on both the Christopher Ironside and Shield 50ps, created coins with the appearance of doubled detail, but with letters overlaying the centre of letters.

This is usually a sign of die fatigue, which does not add any value and is not classed as an error.

The effects of die fatigue are normally difficult to see with the naked eye, the effect shown here can only be seen clearly when magnified.

Missing Design Elements

Also known as: Die Fouling

UK Error Type Rank: 26

Severity
Rarity
Desirability

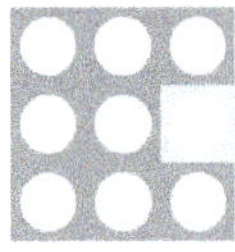

SRD Score: 8 / 30

Coins where part of the design is missing or appears weak, may have been struck with a die where some recesses have become filled with grease or other material.

Die fouling, as it is often referred to, can occur during operation of the press – any foreign matter can plug the cavities into which the planchet's metal would normally flow freely under the striking pressure.

Where only some design elements are missing from part of the coin, take a very close look to ensure it looks right - as detail can be removed from a coin using abrasive substances or materials.

Similar Errors: Weak Strike – can look like die fouling but normally the whole design and edge of both sides is affected in some way.

Value Range: £2 - £20

Weak Strike

Also known as: Die Adjustment Strike

Nations of the Crown £1 Coin; Die Adjustment / Weak Strike

UK Error Type Rank: 27

Severity
Rarity
Desirability

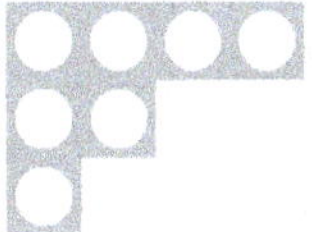

SRD Score: 7 / 30

The die strike force was not sufficient to make a full imprint of the design on the blank. As a result there is often no raised edge on these coins.

Where a coin displays an all over lack of detail, it is not possible to determine the reason by looking at the coin. Whilst die adjustments do take place to set the striking press dies close to the optimum position, these resulting coins from tests would nearly always be removed and recycled.

In my opinion the term "Die Adjustment Strike" is an overused and misleading term, unless you were there at the time of striking, there is no way to know for sure if a coin was the result of a die adjustment test, or simply a weak strike due to a machine issue.

There are large numbers of Weak Strike 2018 Representation of the People Act 50ps – there are quite a few coin press issues that can result in a weak strike, but in reality the cause is not important.

Similar Errors: Missing Design Elements – can look like a weak strike but normally only part of the coin is affected as some die detail is blocked with grease or other material building up on the die.

Value Range: £1 - £20

Most examples are not particularly appealing to look at, weak strikes do not command much of a premium.

If the coin looks like it could have been the result of Die Adjustment Strike, like the £1 coin in the main image - it would be expected to achieve a higher price than a "normal" Weak Strike such as The Representation of the People Act 50p.

Error Type Examples:

10p Weak Strike

5p Weak Strike

The 5p obverse shown above does display similarities to a Missing Design Elements (Die Fouling) error - but there is a very weak non raised edge on both sides, which is consistent with a weak strike. It is also common to see some letters very faint / not fully formed on the obverse of weak strikes.

Blank / Un-struck Planchet

Blanks for 20p, 10p, 5p, 2p, 1p (from left to right, 20p blank is round not shaped like the 50p blank)

UK Error Type Rank: 28

Severity
Rarity
Desirability

SRD Score: 7 / 30

A blank either missed the strike process or a strike was never attempted and it ended up with the struck coins by mistake.

Technically not an error coin, as it is just a blank piece of metal that was intended to be used to make a coin.

It could be considered an error of the process and as such is still collectible.

A Blank that accidentally enters circulation is likely to never be given in change as it is not valid currency.

You may find a blank if you collect sealed bags from a bank or Post Office, but they are uncommon.

Value Range: £1 - £15

A blank that doesn't have any real connection to a specific coin will not be worth very much at all, it is just a shaped piece of metal, BUT:

If the blank has shape or characteristics, such as a 50p shape or bi-metal parts – these will attract more interest as the intended denomination is clear to see.

A blank that went some way to becoming a coin would be of interest to error coin collectors – if the edge inscription has been added, then we have more than a blank – we would know the intended coin design and perhaps even the year.

Coin Hunting in 2024 and beyond

Many people collect what they call picture coins, the commemorative designs that are normally less common than the definitive UK coins, such as the Britannia and Shield 50p.

Some of the commemorative designs are worth more than face value, as shown in the "UK Coin Denominations" sections for the 50p, £2 and 10p coins. For the latest information about which UK coins found in change are the most valuable, visit the Coin Hunter website or download the app.

What is a Bank Run?

People looking to check more than just their change can ask for bags of coins from their bank or any Post Office.

In America, it is known as Coin Roll Hunting, as coins returning to or entering circulation for the first time are packaged in paper rolls of the same denomination coins.

Here in the UK it is very similar, but we currently use plastic bags for coin distribution. UK Coin Hunters can request single denomination bags of coins.

The UK's most collected denomination is the 50 Pence, each small bag of 50ps contains £10 in face value, so 20 coins. There are 25 small bags in a large bank bag, so £250 in value (500 50p coins).

Coin Bag Denominations

Denomination	Small Bag	Large Bank Bag
£2	£20 in value 10 coins	£500 in value 25 small bags / 250 coins
£1	£20 in value 20 coins	£500 in value 25 small bags / 500 coins
50p	£10 in value 20 coins	£250 in value 25 small bags / 500 coins
20p	£10 in value 50 coins	£250 in value 25 small bags / 1250 coins
10p	£5 in value 50 coins	£100 in value 20 small bags / 1000 coins
5p	£5 in value 100 coins	£100 in value 20 small bags / 2000 coins
2p	£1 in value 50 coins	£20 in value 20 small bags / 1000 coins
1p	£1 in value 100 coins	£20 in value 20 small bags / 2000 coins

More coins checked = more chance of finding something of value. This is true, but with so many people now hunting through bags of coins, with each day that passes, more of the desirable coins are removed from circulation.

A bank coin order was placed as research for this book, this included one Large Bank Bag for each denomination from £2 down to 5p. The findings are described in more detail on the following pages.

Is it worth it?

If your goal is financial, to profit from selling coins you find on eBay, it really isn't worth the cost in time. In 2024 there are too few over face value coins left in circulation.

If you enjoy checking coins and the thrill of occasionally finding something for your collection, then give it a go – look at the sort of coins you're finding in the bags from your bank or local Post Office, you can then decide to continue of not.

In 2024 there is a coin surplus due to low demand in recent years. Coins can be stored in cash centres and customer facing financial establishments such as banks for many years untouched.

If you happen across such a store at your local bank, you may find some of the over face value coins listed on the pages that follow.

Large Bank Bags: Personal / Business Bank Accounts

Any Coin Hunter who is polite and friendly to bank and Post Office staff, can normally come away with a few small bags of 50p or £2 coins.

Financial institutions exist to make money from your money, so in a world of free personal banking, it will never be easy to withdraw lots of coins from your bank, check for any good ones and pay the rest back in.

This is because the bank will make no money from fulfilling these 2 time consuming and costly transactions.

BUT: Banks will normally supply full large bank bags of coins to personal customers making a withdrawal from their bank account, the staff member may have a judgemental look on their face as the coins are handed over, they assume you will be selling the over face value coins on eBay and returning the unwanted coins the next day.

Bank staff may refuse your polite request, if they feel the branch doesn't have sufficient stock to ensure coins are always available for paying business customers.

[**Top Tip**]: It is free to withdraw money using a debit card in a Post Office, and they earn a fee for processing the transaction. Most are then happy to supply the amount withdrawn as coins, just check they have the coin denomination(s) you're looking for, before making the withdrawal.

Also, Post Offices earn money from taking in Royal Mail tracked items (even if you purchased the postage online), if you have a few items to send, take them in at the same time as asking to withdraw some coins, the Post Office staff may appreciate you helping them and perhaps help you with coins in return.

When business customers request full bank bags, such as £250 in 50ps or £500 in £2 coins, they are charged for withdrawing coins. The lowest fees are at about 1%, but this may be charged on the amount withdrawn and again on the amount paid back in.

As already mentioned, there are now fewer coins of value left to find – it is not uncommon to see full £250 bags of new to circulation Shield 50ps or already searched bags of old coins with nothing but definitive designs.

This is why ordering coins using a business account is not viable today, costs are very likely to exceed any returns.

The only real advantage of a business account, is the ability to pre order very large quantities as a new coin is released into circulation.

Embracing Change

Having read the last few pages, you may feel that the days of finding anything new or exciting in change or bags of coins are far behind us.

Today it is very hard to build a collection of coins that includes the lower mintage and older mid mintage designs, but there are still opportunities if you change your approach.

If you're already following the standard advice of:

Paying with cash where you can, to leave a known amount of change that can only be given as coins. Chatting to friendly shop staff about collecting coins, to see if they will keep back any special ones they find for you.

What more can you do? - Think about coin distribution and movement.

Right now there is about 90 million pounds worth of coins in long storage at The Royal Mint, when or if needed, these coins will be moved to cash centres.

There are also billions of coins in cash centres around the UK, cages full of large coin bags have sat gathering dust for many years, again, this will only move to banks and Post Offices based on demand.

Less demand for coins means that large stocks just stay where they are, as there is enough to fulfil demand already available.

As a result, Coin Hunters between them are often checking the same coins over and over again – the coins that are figuratively speaking "top of the pile" in banks and Post Offices.

Coins normally join the top of the pile from one of two routes, new coins being forced into circulation and old coins coming back into circulation from home stockpiles or collections.

[**Top Tip**]: Timing can be important, keep an eye on eBay for new coin sealed bag listings, they tend to appear on the same day as a new coin enters circulation.

If you request coin bags as new coins are issued, you will have a chance of finding full sealed bags of brand new coins.

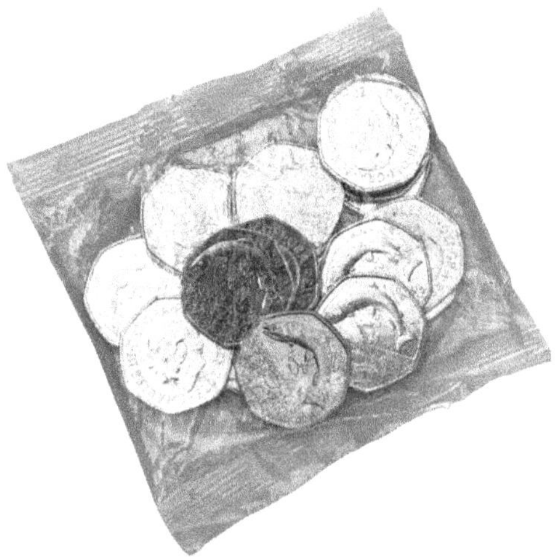

Withdrawing coins from a bank towards the end of the month (when money can be tight) may increase your chances of finding coins from a cashed in collection.

If you're finding no coins for your collection and haven't seen a coin worth over face value for weeks, try other local banks and Post Offices, they may have stocks of older dated bags, for example a "bank bag" with a date sealed of 2019 is much more likely to contain desirable coins from 2018, than a bag dated 2024.

The coin order placed as research for this book included a £100 bank bag of 10ps – it was stamped with a date in March 2019, it contained a single A-Z 10p (2018 A for Angel of the North). The A-Z 10ps were very low mintage when issued, 6 years later you would have close to no chance of finding any A-Z 10p in 2024 dated bags.

UK Coin Denominations

The "top of the pile" bags of the popular denominations, 50p and £2 coins are now nearly all the definitive coin designs, having been picked dry by other Coin Hunters over the years.

At this point in the book, I will assume you have a much better knowledge of error coins to look out for. This can help you find coins worth more than face value, that very few people are looking for.

As we have already seen, there are definitive 50p and £2 coin errors to find – but there will be errors in other denomination bags, such as 20p and 10ps.

Denomination	Alloy	Diameter	Weight
£2	Outer: Nickel-brass Inner: Cupro-nickel	28.4mm	12g
£1	Outer: Nickel-brass Inner: Nickel plated brass alloy	23.43mm	8.75g
50p	Cupro-nickel	27.3mm	8g
20p	Cupro-nickel	21.4mm	5g
10p	Nickel-plated steel	24.5mm	6.5g
5p	Nickel-plated steel	18mm	3.25g
2p	Copper-plated steel	25.9mm	7.12g
1p	Copper-plated steel	20.3mm	3.56g

Coin Hunting for rarer coins and errors by denomination, starting with the 50p and covering UK £2, 10p, £1, 20p, 5p, 2p and 1p coins.

50p Coin Hunting

If you're hunting though a bag of 50p coins, firstly there are a number of commemorative designs to look out for, all designs in circulation are shown on the next pages in highest value first order.

Many of the more severe errors seen on 50p coins will have been spotted and removed from circulation, but there are error coins that remain in circulation for many years.

Error Checking a 50p Coin

At first glance, do both sides look normal? This will pick up most 50p errors, but here are some errors / specific coins to take a second look at.

Known Errors to Double Check:

Check for rotation errors. Check 2017 Benjamin Bunny and 2006 Britannia for 50° (1 side) die rotation.

If the design position does not match the 50p shape, it will be a Collar Rotation Error if both sides are the same amount out of line. See the Collar Error section for more detail.

2016 Jemima Puddle-Duck and 2017 Sir Isaac Newton: Check for die clash error.

Card colour indicates rarity based on circulation mintage figures published by The Royal Mint.

Mintage <1m	Mintage 1m-1.25m	Mintage 1.25m-1.5m	Mintage 1.5m-1.75m	Mintage 1.75m-2.5m	Mintage 2.5m-4m	Mintage 4m-5m	Mintage 5m-6m	Mintage 6m-7m	Mintage Unknown or >7m

*Value Note 1: The 2023 Atlantic Salmon 50p entered circulation in November 2023, this may have been a first batch release. At the time of going to press, the guide value was £8, please check before buying or selling as this valuation is classed as volatile.

*Value Note 2: Coins shown as "Effectively Face Value" can sell for a bit over Face Value, but there would be little to no profit after selling costs.

£140

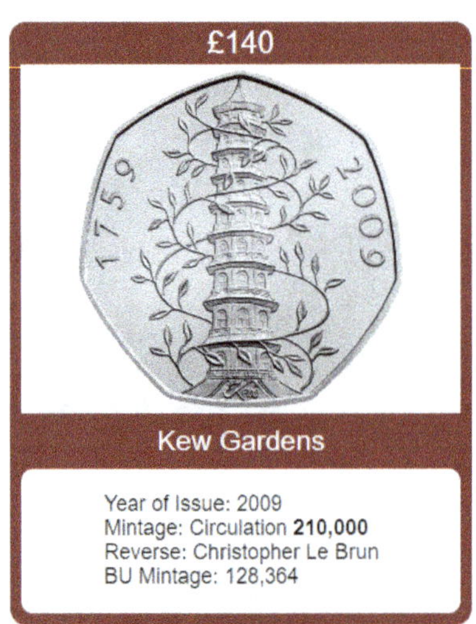

Kew Gardens

Year of Issue: 2009
Mintage: Circulation **210,000**
Reverse: Christopher Le Brun
BU Mintage: 128,364

£13

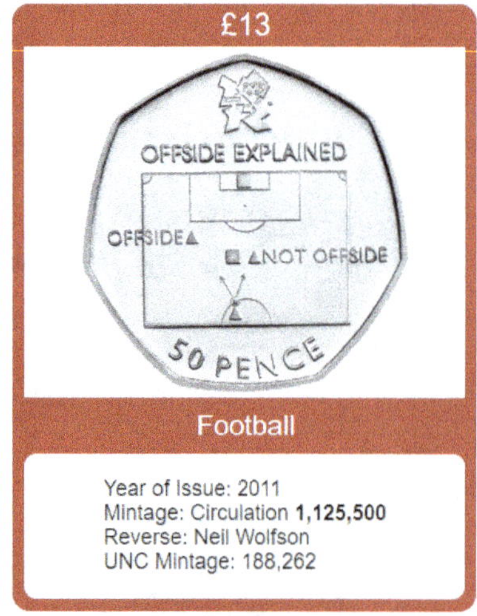

Football

Year of Issue: 2011
Mintage: Circulation **1,125,500**
Reverse: Neil Wolfson
UNC Mintage: 188,262

£10.50

Triathlon

Year of Issue: 2011
Mintage: Circulation **1,163,500**
Reverse: Sarah Harvey
UNC Mintage: 146,354

£10

Judo

Year of Issue: 2011
Mintage: Circulation **1,161,500**
Reverse: David Cornell
UNC Mintage: 128,442

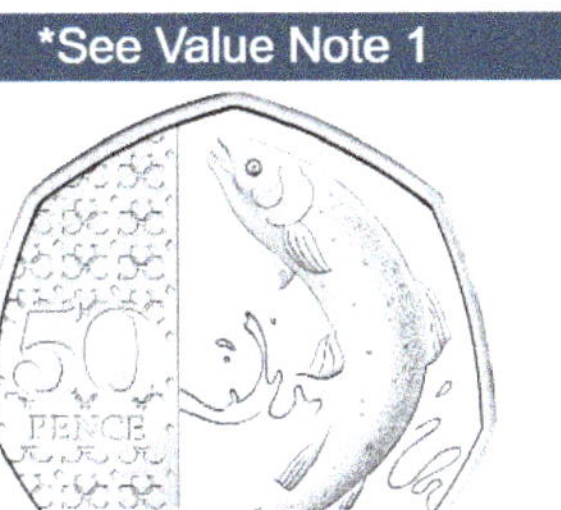

Atlantic Salmon

*See Value Note 1

Year of Issue: 2023
Mintage: Circulation Unknown
Reverse: The Royal Mint
BU Mintage: 0

Wrestling

£7.50

Year of Issue: 2011
Mintage: Circulation **1,129,500**
Reverse: Roderick Enriquez
BU Mintage: 127,279

Jemima Puddle-Duck

£7

Year of Issue: 2016
Mintage: Circulation **2,100,000**
Reverse: Emma Noble
BU Mintage: 138,937

Peter Rabbit

£4.50

Year of Issue: 2018
Mintage: Circulation **1,400,000**
Reverse: Emma Noble
BU Mintage: 163,403

Flopsy Bunny

£4.50

Year of Issue: 2018
Mintage: Circulation **1,400,000**
Reverse: Emma Noble
BU Mintage: 132,759

Mrs Tittlemouse

£3

Year of Issue: 2018
Mintage: Circulation **1,700,000**
Reverse: Emma Noble
BU Mintage: 130,385

<table>
<tr><td>

£2.50

Shooting

Year of Issue: 2011
Mintage: Circulation **1,656,500**
Reverse: Pravin Dewdhory
UNC Mintage: 125,398

</td><td>

£2.50

Tennis

Year of Issue: 2011
Mintage: Circulation **1,454,000**
Reverse: Tracy Baines
UNC Mintage: 144,535

</td></tr>
<tr><td>

£2.50

Sir Isaac Newton

Year of Issue: 2017
Mintage: Circulation **1,801,500**
Reverse: Aaron West
BU Mintage: 98,294

</td><td>

£2.25

Hockey

Year of Issue: 2011
Mintage: Circulation **1,773,500**
Reverse: Robert Evans
UNC Mintage: 130,813

</td></tr>
<tr><td>

£2.25

Sailing

Year of Issue: 2011
Mintage: Circulation **1,749,500**
Reverse: Bruce Rushin
UNC Mintage: 138,535

</td><td>

£2

Suffragettes

Year of Issue: 2003
Mintage: Circulation **3,124,030**
Reverse: Mary Milner Dickens
BU Mintage: 122,581

</td></tr>
</table>

£2

50 PENCE

Aquatics

Year of Issue: 2011
Mintage: Circulation **2,179,000**
Reverse: Jonathan Olliffe
UNC Mintage: 157,990

£2

50 PENCE

Athletics

Year of Issue: 2011
Mintage: Circulation **2,224,000**
Reverse: Florence Jackson
UNC Mintage: 168,498

£2

50 PENCE

Basketball

Year of Issue: 2011
Mintage: Circulation **1,748,000**
Reverse: Sarah Payne
UNC Mintage: 137,157

£2

50 PENCE

Boccia

Year of Issue: 2011
Mintage: Circulation **2,166,000**
Reverse: Justin Chung
UNC Mintage: 126,662

£2

50 PENCE

Goalball

Year of Issue: 2011
Mintage: Circulation **1,615,500**
Reverse: Jonathan Wren
UNC Mintage: 114,334

£2

50 PENCE

Gymnastics

Year of Issue: 2011
Mintage: Circulation **1,720,813**
Reverse: Jonathan Olliffe
UNC Mintage: 145,895

£2

Handball

Year of Issue: 2011
Mintage: Circulation **1,676,500**
Reverse: Natasha Ratcliffe
UNC Mintage: 117,566

£2

Modern Pentathlon

Year of Issue: 2011
Mintage: Circulation **1,689,500**
Reverse: Daniel Brittain
UNC Mintage: 123,357

£2

Rowing

Year of Issue: 2011
Mintage: Circulation **1,717,300**
Reverse: Davey Podmore
UNC Mintage: 140,977

£2

Table Tennis

Year of Issue: 2011
Mintage: Circulation **1,737,500**
Reverse: Alan Linsdell
UNC Mintage: 123,195

£2

Taekwondo

Year of Issue: 2011
Mintage: Circulation **1,664,000**
Reverse: David Gibbons
UNC Mintage: 120,210

£2

Weightlifting

Year of Issue: 2011
Mintage: Circulation **1,879,500**
Reverse: Rob Shakespeare
UNC Mintage: 121,778

£2

Wheelchair Rugby

Year of Issue: 2011
Mintage: Circulation **1,765,500**
Reverse: Natasha Ratcliffe
UNC Mintage: 121,175

£1.75

WWF

Year of Issue: 2011
Mintage: Circulation **3,400,000**
Reverse: Matthew Dent
BU Mintage: 67,299

£1.50

European Union

Year of Issue: 1998
Mintage: Circulation **5,043,000**
Reverse: John Mills
BU Mintage: 147,883

£1.50

NHS

Year of Issue: 1998
Mintage: Circulation **5,001,000**
Reverse: David Cornell
BU Mintage: 50,894

£1.50

Badminton

Year of Issue: 2011
Mintage: Circulation **2,133,500**
Reverse: Emma Kelly
UNC Mintage: 124,237

£1.50

Boxing

Year of Issue: 2011
Mintage: Circulation **2,148,500**
Reverse: Shane Abery
UNC Mintage: 142,151

£1.50

Canoeing

Year of Issue: 2011
Mintage: Circulation **2,166,500**
Reverse: Timothy Lees
UNC Mintage: 116,114

£1.50

Cycling

Year of Issue: 2011
Mintage: Circulation **2,090,500**
Reverse: Theo Crutchley-Mack
UNC Mintage: 156,872

£1.50

Equestrian

Year of Issue: 2011
Mintage: Circulation **2,142,500**
Reverse: Thomas Babbage
UNC Mintage: 145,122

£1.50

Fencing

Year of Issue: 2011
Mintage: Circulation **2,115,500**
Reverse: Ruth Summerfield
UNC Mintage: 130,815

£1.50

Volleyball

Year of Issue: 2011
Mintage: Circulation **2,133,500**
Reverse: Daniela Boothman
UNC Mintage: 124,115

£1.25

The Tailor of Gloucester

Year of Issue: 2018
Mintage: Circulation **3,900,000**
Reverse: Emma Noble
BU Mintage: 136,357

£1 (Effectively Face Value)

Archery

Year of Issue: 2011
Mintage: Circulation **3,345,500**
Reverse: Piotr Powaga
UNC Mintage: 140,195

£1 (Effectively Face Value)

Benjamin Britten

Year of Issue: 2013
Mintage: Circulation **5,300,000**
Reverse: Tom Phillips CBE RA
BU Mintage: 13,337

£1 (Effectively Face Value)

Battle of Britain

Year of Issue: 2015
Mintage: Circulation **5,900,000**
Reverse: Gary Breeze
BU Mintage: 0

£1 (Effectively Face Value)

Battle of Hastings

Year of Issue: 2016
Mintage: Circulation **6,700,000**
Reverse: John Bergdahl
BU Mintage: 57,520

£1 (Effectively Face Value)

Beatrix Potter Anniversary

Year of Issue: 2016
Mintage: Circulation **6,900,000**
Reverse: Emma Noble
BU Mintage: 125,085

£1 (Effectively Face Value)

Peter Rabbit

Year of Issue: 2016
Mintage: Circulation **9,700,000**
Reverse: Emma Noble
BU Mintage: 151,012

£1 (Effectively Face Value)

Team GB

Year of Issue: 2016
Mintage: Circulation **6,400,000**
Reverse: Tim Sharp
BU Mintage: 42,646

£1 (Effectively Face Value)

Squirrel Nutkin

Year of Issue: 2016
Mintage: Circulation **5,000,000**
Reverse: Emma Noble
BU Mintage: 114,321

£1 (Effectively Face Value)

Mrs Tiggy-Winkle

Year of Issue: 2016
Mintage: Circulation **8,800,000**
Reverse: Emma Noble
BU Mintage: 115,311

£1 (Effectively Face Value)

Paddington at the Station

Year of Issue: 2018
Mintage: Circulation **5,001,000**
Reverse: David Knapton
BU Mintage: 174,546

£1 (Effectively Face Value)

Paddington at the Palace

Year of Issue: 2018
Mintage: Circulation **5,901,000**
Reverse: David Knapton
BU Mintage: 149,842

£1 (Effectively Face Value)

King Charles III Coronation

Year of Issue: 2023
Mintage: Circulation **5,000,000**
Reverse: Natasha Jenkins
BU Mintage: 0

Britannia

Years of Issue: 1997 - 2008
Mintage: Circulation **805,926,100**
Reverse: Christopher Ironside

Public Libraries

Year of Issue: 2000
Mintage: Circulation **11,263,000**
Reverse: Mary Milner Dickens
BU Mintage: 184,294

Roger Bannister

Year of Issue: 2004
Mintage: Circulation **9,032,500**
Reverse: James Butler
BU Mintage: 109,379

Dictionary

Year of Issue: 2005
Mintage: Circulation **17,649,000**
Reverse: Tom Phillips
BU Mintage: 92,522

Victoria Cross heroic acts

Year of Issue: 2006
Mintage: Circulation **10,000,500**
Reverse: Clive Duncan
BU Mintage: 131,375

Victoria Cross medal

Year of Issue: 2006
Mintage: Circulation **12,087,000**
Reverse: Claire Aldridge
BU Mintage: 137,285

Scouting

Year of Issue: 2007
Mintage: Circulation **7,710,750**
Reverse: Kerry Jones
BU Mintage: 138,510

Shield of the Royal Arms

Years of Issue: 2008 - 2022
Mintage: Circulation **353,590,405**
Reverse: Matthew Dent

Girlguiding

Year of Issue: 2010
Mintage: Circulation **7,410,090**
Reverse: Jonathan Evans and Donna Hainan
BU Mintage: 99,075

Christopher Ironside

Year of Issue: 2013
Mintage: Circulation **7,000,000**
Reverse: Christopher Ironside
BU Mintage: 17,906

Glasgow Commonwealth Games

Year of Issue: 2014
Mintage: Circulation **6,500,000**
Reverse: Alex Loudon with Dan Flashman
BU Mintage: 36,364

Peter Rabbit

Year of Issue: 2017
Mintage: Circulation **19,900,000**
Reverse: Emma Noble
BU Mintage: 223,661

Face Value

Jeremy Fisher

Year of Issue: 2017
Mintage: Circulation **9,900,000**
Reverse: Emma Noble
BU Mintage: 167,160

Face Value

Tom Kitten

Year of Issue: 2017
Mintage: Circulation **9,500,000**
Reverse: Emma Noble
BU Mintage: 160,496

Face Value

Benjamin Bunny

Year of Issue: 2017
Mintage: Circulation **25,000,000**
Reverse: Emma Noble
BU Mintage: 160,040

Face Value

Representation of the People Act

Year of Issue: 2018
Mintage: Circulation **9,000,000**
Reverse: Stephen Taylor
BU Mintage: 71,128

Face Value

Sherlock Holmes

Year of Issue: 2019
Mintage: Circulation **8,602,000**
Reverse: Stephen Raw
BU Mintage: 111,805

Face Value

Paddington at the Tower

Year of Issue: 2019
Mintage: Circulation **9,001,000**
Reverse: David Knapton
BU Mintage: 87,965

Paddington at St Paul's

Year of Issue: 2019
Mintage: Circulation **9,001,000**
Reverse: David Knapton
BU Mintage: 83,718

Brexit

Year of Issue: 2020
Mintage: Circulation **10,001,000**
BU Mintage: 308,362

Diversity built Britain

Year of Issue: 2020
Mintage: Circulation **10,300,000**
Reverse: Dominique Evans
BU Mintage: 65,517

Platinum Jubilee

Year of Issue: 2022
Mintage: Circulation **5,000,070**
Reverse: Osborne Ross

Pride

Year of Issue: 2022
Mintage: Circulation **5,000,000**
Reverse: Dominique Holmes

Queen Elizabeth II Memorial

Year of Issue: 2022
Mintage: Circulation **9,600,000**
Reverse: Edgar Fuller & Cecil Thomas

£2 Coin Hunting

When hunting though bags of £2 coins, check for commemorative designs worth more than face value, the list on the next page shows all circulation designs in highest value first order.

Errors like Offset Centre Insert and Struck on Un-punched Planchet are only seen on bi-metal coins, you would need to be very lucky to find one of these. It is worth checking £2 coins for errors that most people will not see, as small errors that are relatively common on £2s can make the coin collectible and worth more than face value.

Error Checking a £2 Coin

Do both sides look normal? Turn the coin like the page of a book to check for rotation.

Check all £2 coins for Die Break errors, pay close attention to Technology £2 coins, especially near the edge of the coin and within the cross patterned outer border.

Here are some specific coins to take a second look at.

Known Errors to Double Check:

2010 Technology: Check for the Die Doubling Error.

2014 First World War Centenary: Check for the No Denomination Mule error.

2015 First World War Navy: Check for the Flag Die Break error.

2016 Shakespeare Tragedies: Check for the Wrong Edge Inscription error: "FOR KING AND COUNTRY".

Card colour indicates rarity based on circulation mintage figures published by The Royal Mint.

*Value Note 1: Coins shown as "Effectively Face Value" can sell for a bit over Face Value, but there would be little to no profit after selling costs.

£32

Commonwealth Games - Northern Ireland

Year of Issue: 2002
Mintage: Circulation **485,500**
Reverse: Matthew Bonaccorsi
BU Mintage: 18,812
Edge: SPIRIT OF
FRIENDSHIP,MANCHESTER 2002

£13

Commonwealth Games - Wales

Year of Issue: 2002
Mintage: Circulation **588,500**
Reverse: Matthew Bonaccorsi
BU Mintage: 18,812
Edge: SPIRIT OF
FRIENDSHIP,MANCHESTER 2002

£10

Commonwealth Games - England

Year of Issue: 2002
Mintage: Circulation **650,500**
Reverse: Matthew Bonaccorsi
BU Mintage: 18,812
Edge: SPIRIT OF
FRIENDSHIP,MANCHESTER 2002

£8.50

Commonwealth Games - Scotland

Year of Issue: 2002
Mintage: Circulation **771,750**
Reverse: Matthew Bonaccorsi
BU Mintage: 18,812
Edge: SPIRIT OF
FRIENDSHIP,MANCHESTER 2002

£5

Olympic Games Handover to Rio

Year of Issue: 2012
Mintage: Circulation **845,000**
Reverse: Jonathan Olliffe
BU Mintage: 28,356
Edge: I CALL UPON THE YOUTH OF THE WORLD

£4

Olympic Games Handover to London

Year of Issue: 2008
Mintage: Circulation **918,000**
Reverse: Thomas T Docherty
BU Mintage: 57,346
Edge: I CALL UPON THE YOUTH OF THE WORLD

£4

Olympic Games of 1908

Year of Issue: 2008
Mintage: Circulation **910,000**
Reverse: The Royal Mint Engraving Team
BU Mintage: 109,044
Edge: THE 4TH OLYMPIAD LONDON

£4

King James Bible

Year of Issue: 2011
Mintage: Circulation **975,000**
Reverse: Paul Stafford & Benjamin Wright
BU Mintage: 70,226
Edge: THE AUTHORISED VERSION

£4

Mary Rose

Year of Issue: 2011
Mintage: Circulation **1,040,000**
Reverse: John Bergdahl
BU Mintage: 67,298
Edge: YOUR NOBLEST SHIPPE 1511

£4

Britannia

Year of Issue: 2021
Mintage: Circulation **6,045,000**
Reverse: Antony Dufort
BU Mintage: 45,070
Edge: QUATUOR MARIA VINDICO
Not yet in circulation

£4

Britannia

Year of Issue: 2022
Mintage: Circulation **4,030,000**
Reverse: Antony Dufort
Edge: QUATUOR MARIA VINDICO
Not yet in circulation

£3

London Underground Train

Year of Issue: 2013
Mintage: Circulation **1,690,000**
Reverse: Edward Barber and Jay Osgerby
BU Mintage: 34,400
Edge: Linear representation of the Tube map

£3

London Underground Roundel

Year of Issue: 2013
Mintage: Circulation **1,560,000**
Reverse: Edwina Ellis
BU Mintage: 34,400
Edge: MIND THE GAP

£3

First World War Centenary Navy

Year of Issue: 2015
Mintage: Circulation **650,000**
Reverse: David Rowlands
BU Mintage: 0
Edge: THE SURE SHIELD OF BRITAIN

£3

Britannia

Year of Issue: 2015
Mintage: Circulation **650,000**
Reverse: Antony Dufort
BU Mintage: 40,882
Edge: QUATUOR MARIA VINDICO

£2.50 (Effectively Face Value)

Magna Carta

Year of Issue: 2015
Mintage: Circulation **1,495,000**
Reverse: John Bergdahl
BU Mintage: 0
Edge: FOUNDATION OF LIBERTY

Shakespeare Tragedies

Year of Issue: 2016
Mintage: Circulation **4,615,000**
Reverse: John Bergdahl
BU Mintage: 60,807
Edge: WHAT A PIECE OF WORK IS A MAN

Great Fire of London

Year of Issue: 2016
Mintage: Circulation **1,625,000**
Reverse: Aaron West
BU Mintage: 59,382
Edge: THE WHOLE CITY IN DREADFUL FLAMES

Face Value

Technology

Years of Issue: 1997 - 2015
Mintage: Circulation **416,145,838**
Reverse: Bruce Rushin
Edge: STANDING ON THE SHOULDERS OF GIANTS

Face Value

Rugby World Cup

Year of Issue: 1999
Mintage: Circulation **4,933,000**
Reverse: Ron Dutton
BU Mintage: 201,817
Edge: Rugby World Cup 1999

Face Value

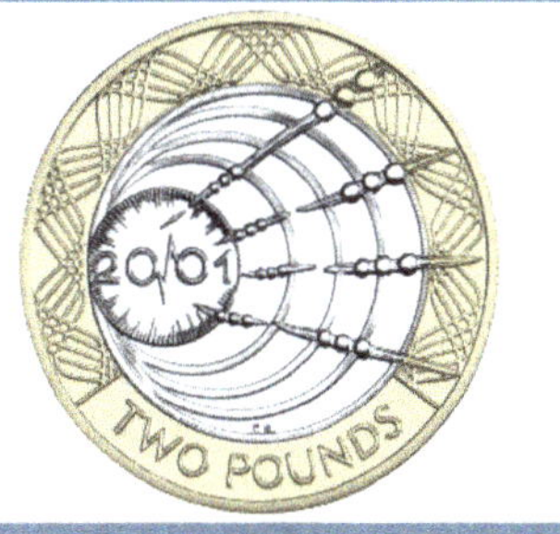

Wireless Transmission

Year of Issue: 2001
Mintage: Circulation **4,558,000**
Reverse: Robert Evans
BU Mintage: 151,367
Edge: WIRELESS BRIDGES THE ATLANTIC...MARCONI 1901...

Face Value

Discovery of DNA

Year of Issue: 2003
Mintage: Circulation **4,299,000**
Reverse: John Mills
BU Mintage: 149,354
Edge: DEOXYRIBONUCLEIC ACID

Steam Locomotive

Year of Issue: 2004
Mintage: Circulation **5,004,500**
Reverse: Robert Lowe
BU Mintage: 155,879
Edge: Is milled with an incuse railway line motif.

End of World War II

Year of Issue: 2005
Mintage: Circulation **10,191,000**
Reverse: Bob Elderton
BU Mintage: 53,686
Edge: In Victory Magnanimity in Peace Goodwill

Gunpowder Plot

Year of Issue: 2005
Mintage: Circulation **5,140,500**
Reverse: Peter Forster
BU Mintage: 104,566
Edge: REMEMBER REMEMBER FIFTH OF NOVEMBER

Brunel Portrait

Year of Issue: 2006
Mintage: Circulation **7,928,250**
Reverse: Rod Kelly
BU Mintage: 172,685
Edge: 1806-1859 ISAMBARD KINGDOM BRUNEL ENGINEER

Brunel Paddington Station

Year of Issue: 2006
Mintage: Circulation **7,452,250**
Reverse: Robert Evans
BU Mintage: 130,815
Edge: SO MANY IRONS IN THE FIRE

Act of Union

Year of Issue: 2007
Mintage: Circulation **7,545,000**
Reverse: Yvonne Holton
BU Mintage: 109,241
Edge: UNITED INTO ONE KINGDOM

Face Value

Slave Trade

Year of Issue: 2007
Mintage: Circulation **8,445,000**
Reverse: David Gentleman
BU Mintage: 0
Edge: AM I NOT A MAN AND A BROTHER

Face Value

Robert Burns

Year of Issue: 2009
Mintage: Circulation **3,253,000**
Reverse: The Royal Mint Engraving Team
BU Mintage: 120,023
Edge: SHOULD AULD ACQUAINTANCE BE FORGOT

Face Value

Charles Darwin

Year of Issue: 2009
Mintage: Circulation **3,903,000**
Reverse: Suzie Zamit
BU Mintage: 115,839
Edge: ON THE ORIGIN OF SPECIES 1859

Face Value

Florence Nightingale

Year of Issue: 2010
Mintage: Circulation **6,175,000**
Reverse: Gordon Summers
BU Mintage: 79,323
Edge: 150 YEARS OF NURSING

Face Value

Charles Dickens

Year of Issue: 2012
Mintage: Circulation **8,190,000**
Reverse: Matthew Dent
BU Mintage: 100,486
Edge: SOMETHING WILL TURN UP

Face Value

Anniversary of the Guinea

Year of Issue: 2013
Mintage: Circulation **2,990,000**
Reverse: Anthony Smith ARBS
BU Mintage: 23,843
Edge: WHAT IS A GUINEA? 'TIS A SPLENDID THING

First World War Centenary

Year of Issue: 2014
Mintage: Circulation **5,720,000**
Reverse: John Bergdahl
BU Mintage: 64,712
Edge: THE LAMPS ARE GOING OUT ALL OVER EUROPE

Trinity House

Year of Issue: 2014
Mintage: Circulation **3,705,000**
Reverse: Joe Whitlock Blundell & David Eccles
BU Mintage: 31,386
Edge: SERVING THE MARINER

Shakespeare Histories

Year of Issue: 2016
Mintage: Circulation **5,655,000**
Reverse: John Bergdahl
BU Mintage: 60,648
Edge: THE HOLLOW CROWN

Shakespeare Comedies

Year of Issue: 2016
Mintage: Circulation **4,355,000**
Reverse: John Bergdahl
BU Mintage: 57,807
Edge: ALL THE WORLDS A STAGE

First World War Centenary Army

Year of Issue: 2016
Mintage: Circulation **9,550,000**
Reverse: Tim Sharp
BU Mintage: 50,047
Edge: FOR KING AND COUNTRY

Britannia

Year of Issue: 2016
Mintage: Circulation **2,925,000**
Reverse: Antony Dufort
BU Mintage: 38,502
Edge: QUATUOR MARIA VINDICO

10p Coin Hunting

If you're hunting though a bag of 10p coins, there are 26 A to Z designs to look out for, these are shown on this page and the next four pages.

Error Checking a 10p Coin

At first glance, do both sides look normal?, turn the coin like the page of a book to check for rotation.

Check all 10p coins for Die Break errors, pay close attention to Shield 10p coins, especially near the edge of the coin close to the lions.

Red Outline: 2011 Shield 10p Cud and Die Break map with positions, shapes and sizes seen on 2011 to 2104 coins.

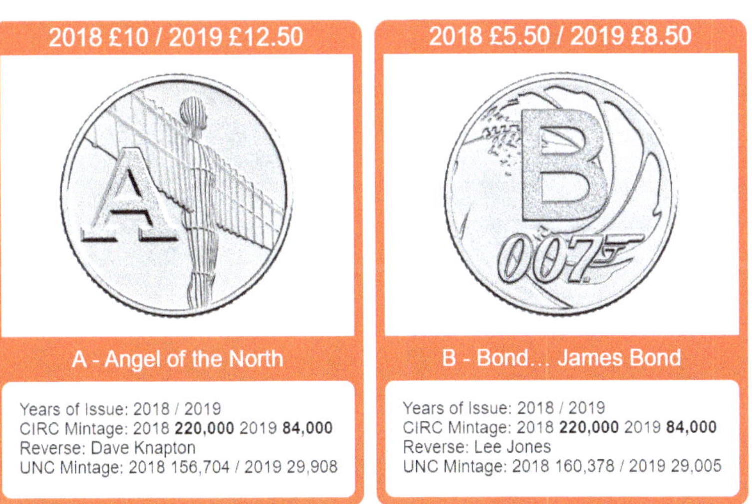

C - Cricket

Years of Issue: 2018 / 2019
CIRC Mintage: 2018 **220,000** 2019 **84,000**
Reverse: The Royal Mint Team
UNC Mintage: 2018 143,363 / 2019 29,779

D - Double Decker Bus

Years of Issue: 2018 / 2019
CIRC Mintage: 2018 **220,000** 2019 **84,000**
Reverse: The Royal Mint Team
UNC Mintage: 2018 137,475 / 2019 27,669

E - English Breakfast

Years of Issue: 2018 / 2019
CIRC Mintage: 2018 **220,000** 2019 **84,000**
Reverse: Dave Knapton
UNC Mintage: 2018 148,264 / 2019 29,276

F - Fish and Chips

Years of Issue: 2018 / 2019
CIRC Mintage: 2018 **220,000** 2019 **84,000**
Reverse: The Royal Mint Team
UNC Mintage: 2018 134,048 / 2019 26,291

G - Greenwich Mean Time

Years of Issue: 2018 / 2019
CIRC Mintage: 2018 **220,000** 2019 **84,000**
Reverse: The Royal Mint Team
UNC Mintage: 2018 131,133 / 2019 25,960

H - Houses of Parliament

Years of Issue: 2018 / 2019
CIRC Mintage: 2018 **220,000** 2019 **84,000**
Reverse: The Royal Mint Team
UNC Mintage: 2018 135,933 / 2019 27,304

2018 £2.50 / 2019 £3.50

I - Ice-Cream Cone

Years of Issue: 2018 / 2019
CIRC Mintage: 2018 **220,000** 2019 **84,000**
Reverse: Dave Knapton
UNC Mintage: 2018 147,505 / 2019 27,699

2018 £2.25 / 2019 £3.50

K - King Arthur

Years of Issue: 2018 / 2019
CIRC Mintage: 2018 **220,000** 2019 **84,000**
Reverse: P J Lynch
UNC Mintage: 2018 136,292 / 2019 26,319

2018 £2.75 / 2019 £3.75

M - Mackintosh

Years of Issue: 2018 / 2019
CIRC Mintage: 2018 **220,000** 2019 **84,000**
Reverse: P J Lynch
UNC Mintage: 2018 139,254 / 2019 27,427

2018 £2.50 / 2019 £3.50

J - Jubilee

Years of Issue: 2018 / 2019
CIRC Mintage: 2018 **220,000** 2019 **84,000**
Reverse: Bradley Morgan Johnson
UNC Mintage: 2018 132,692 / 2019 27,126

2018 £2.50 / 2019 £4

L - Loch Ness Monster

Years of Issue: 2018 / 2019
CIRC Mintage: 2018 **220,000** 2019 **84,000**
Reverse: P J Lynch
UNC Mintage: 2018 146,695 / 2019 29,471

2018 £3.50 / 2019 £4

N - National Health Service

Years of Issue: 2018 / 2019
CIRC Mintage: 2018 **220,000** 2019 **84,000**
Reverse: The Royal Mint Team
UNC Mintage: 2018 148,969 / 2019 29,619

2018 £2.50 / 2019 £3.75

O - Oak Tree

Years of Issue: 2018 / 2019
CIRC Mintage: 2018 **220,000** 2019 **84,000**
Reverse: The Royal Mint Team
UNC Mintage: 2018 139,512 / 2019 27,190

2018 £2.50 / 2019 £3

P - Post Box

Years of Issue: 2018 / 2019
CIRC Mintage: 2018 **220,000** 2019 **84,000**
Reverse: P J Lynch
UNC Mintage: 2018 134,269 / 2019 25,959

2018 £1.75 / 2019 £3

Q - Queuing

Years of Issue: 2018 / 2019
CIRC Mintage: 2018 **220,000** 2019 **83,000**
Reverse: The Royal Mint Team
UNC Mintage: 2018 125,768 / 2019 25,787

2018 £4.75 / 2019 £7.50

R - Robin

Years of Issue: 2018 / 2019
CIRC Mintage: 2018 **220,000** 2019 **64,000**
Reverse: P J Lynch
UNC Mintage: 2018 148,927 / 2019 29,173

2018 £2.50 / 2019 £3.75

S - Stonehenge

Years of Issue: 2018 / 2019
CIRC Mintage: 2018 **220,000** 2019 **84,000**
Reverse: The Royal Mint Team
UNC Mintage: 2018 145,357 / 2019 29,338

2018 £3 / 2019 £3.50

T - Teapot

Years of Issue: 2018 / 2019
CIRC Mintage: 2018 **220,000** 2019 **84,000**
Reverse: The Royal Mint Team
UNC Mintage: 2018 135,254 / 2019 28,105

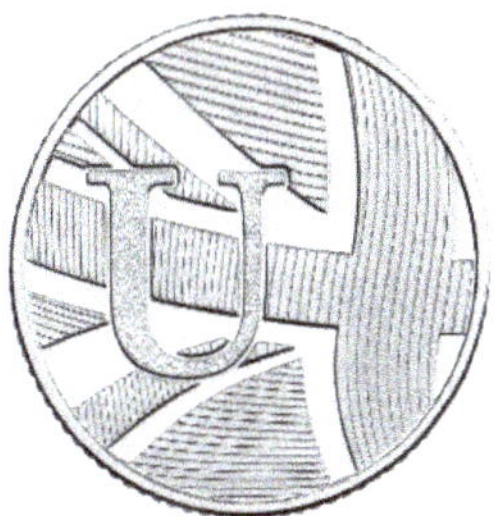

2018 £2 / 2019 £3.25

U - Union Flag

Years of Issue: 2018 / 2019
CIRC Mintage: 2018 **220,000** 2019 **84,000**
Reverse: The Royal Mint Team
UNC Mintage: 2018 134,335 / 2019 26,987

2018 £2.25 / 2019 £3

V - Villages

Years of Issue: 2018 / 2019
CIRC Mintage: 2018 **220,000** 2019 **84,000**
Reverse: P J Lynch
UNC Mintage: 2018 132,236 / 2019 25,695

2018 £2 / 2019 £5

W - World Wide Web

Years of Issue: 2018 / 2019
CIRC Mintage: 2018 **220,000** 2019 **63,000**
Reverse: The Royal Mint Team
UNC Mintage: 2018 133,127 / 2019 26,500

2018 £1.75 / 2019 £3

X - X marks the spot

Years of Issue: 2018 / 2019
CIRC Mintage: 2018 **220,000** 2019 **84,000**
Reverse: P J Lynch
UNC Mintage: 2018 129,117 / 2019 26,058

2018 £2.75 / 2019 £8

Y - Yeoman Warder

Years of Issue: 2018 / 2019
CIRC Mintage: 2018 **220,000** 2019 **63,000**
Reverse: The Royal Mint Team
UNC Mintage: 2018 133,386 / 2019 28,003

2018 £2 / 2019 £7

Z - Zebra Crossing

Years of Issue: 2018 / 2019
CIRC Mintage: 2018 **220,000** 2019 **63,000**
Reverse: Bradley Morgan Johnson
UNC Mintage: 2018 130,751 / 2019 27,076

£1 Coin Hunting

Here we are only looking at coins currently in circulation, at the time of writing every £1 coin that can be found in change features the definitive Nations of the Crown design by David Pearce (who was 15 when the design was drawn).

In May 2022, a new £1 coin design "Culture & Creativity" was introduced without images as the next £1 coin design, we were told it would enter circulation in 2023, 40 years after the first £1 coin was struck.

Plans were changed following the death of Queen Elizabeth II, so the next £1 coin we should see in our change in 2024 is the 2023 dated Bees £1.

Coin Hunters taking on a £500 bag of £1 coins may find it a bit tedious, with just errors to check for and one needing a magnifying glass or a zoomed in phone camera – it is quite hard work.

Error Checking a £1 Coin

At first glance, do both sides look normal?, turn the coin like the page of a book to check for rotation.

The more serious errors such as Struck on Un-punched Planchet and Offset Centre Insert should be very easy to spot, so here are a few known issues with the Nations of the Crown £1 coin that require a closer look.

The image on the left shows a Partial collar error.

The image on the right is a Die Break error, the ring of raised blobs inside the red lines are where the cracks in the die filled with metal as the coin was struck. This error is thought to resemble a crown of thorns.

2016 Mule – check the date micro-lettering on the reverse of 2016 coins, looking for coins showing 2017.

You may have heard the term "Lefty" or Leftie" applied to the 12 sided £1 coin and wondered if this is an error you should be looking out for.

What is a "Lefty"?

A £1 coin has alternate milled and smooth edges on the 12 sides – with most £1 coins produced with the collar in a position so that it starts with a milled edge to the right of the portrait (when heads side is upwards) and ends with a smooth edge to the left.

A "Lefty" is simply a coin where the alternating milled / smooth starts on the left of the portrait – so the side to the left is milled instead of the "normal" smooth. This just means that the collar was installed one side rotated.

This is not an error because the coin specification states: "Milled edges – it has grooves on alternate sides", which is true no matter how the collar is installed.

BUT: Some people do like to collect the different variations, which can mean that some £1 coins do sell for a bit more than face value.

If you do check for Lefties – expect to find lots of 2016 coins with the milling to the left, as in the first year of production it seems the collar was not always put in taking account of the milled / smooth edge positions.

In checking lots of £1 coins it does seem that The Royal Mint have now decided to try and keep the milled / smooth edge position the same for circulation coin production. It can be much harder to find circulation £1 lefties from 2018 on, so it may be worth keeping any non 2016 lefties.

The research test order included a £500 bag of £1 coins, 500 coins in total were checked for Offset Centre Insert, Partial collar errors, Die Breaks and 2016 Mules.

Nothing of note was found, there were 2016 Lefties, but none for any other dates.

New Designs Entering Circulation: A Coin Hunting Opportunity

Soon full bank bags of Bees £1 coins will enter circulation, the more desirable and noticeable errors that have been seen on the Nations of the Crown £1, will no doubt also be seen on the new Bees £1.

The higher value errors such as Struck on Un-punched Planchet, Struck Off-Centre, Struck on Inner / Outer Only, Offset Centre Insert, Double Struck / Multi Struck – will be removed from circulation by the first person to see the coin.

At the point in time when sealed bags first appear for sale on eBay, you can obtain and check new issue coins, so you will be the first person to see the coins.

20p Coin Hunting

The research test order included a £250 bag of 20p coins, 1250 coins in total were checked for errors with a focus on looking for the undated mule 20p and Die Break errors.

115,022,000 2008 Shield 20ps entered circulation, The Royal Mint have estimated that this number included up to 250,000 undated 20ps. This would equate to about 1 in 460 of the Shield 20p coins struck for circulation in 2008.

Anyone aware of this error in 2008 would have had a very good chance of finding hundreds of this very popular error coin.

But since 1982 when the 20p was first struck and the change of design in 2008, over 3 billion 20ps had entered circulation, so finding one in change then would have been a long shot of about 12000/1.

In 2024 your chances of finding this heavily publicised coin in change or bank bags is very small. Since the comparatively small number of undated 20ps entered circulation, over 1.3 billion more have been issued. There is also no doubt that many of the error coins have now been removed from circulation by collectors.

With a realistic estimate of the undated 20p and all other 20ps still in circulation, today you would still do well to find one in 100,000 coins checked (80 full £250 bank bags or £20,000).

So you will not be surprised to know that we did not find an undated 20p in our £250 bag of 20ps, but we did find one Die "Deterioration" error. Not a clean and obvious Die Break, the image on the next page shows raised metal indicative of an overused die.

The 2012 coin we found showed evidence of Die Deterioration at the centre of the portrait on the obverse die.

Error Checking a 20p Coin

At first glance, do both sides look normal?, turn the coin like the page of a book to check for rotation.

Check all 20p coins for Die Break errors, especially around the edge of the reverse and within the portrait on the obverse.

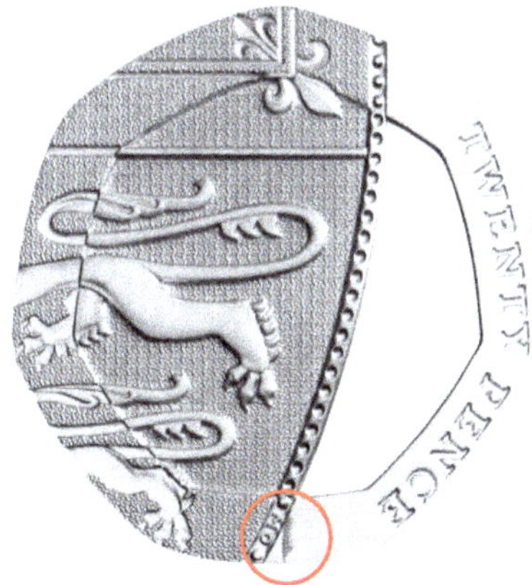

This die break can be found on some 2008 20ps, it looks a bit like an upside down 1.

If you have the coins in hand, you may as well check for the undated 20p mule just in case.

Check for Wrong Planchet as this has been seen on a number of 20p coins – if a blank intended for a different denomination or a foreign coin has been used, it is likely that any non-silver in colour would have already been removed from circulation, BUT 5p and foreign blanks can find there way into the 20p striking process.

To spot Wrong Denomination Planchet / Foreign Planchet errors, look for coins that are thin or feel light – they often have a round side instead of 7 clearly defined sides, as the amount of metal was not enough to reach the edges of the 20p collar.

To check a coin that you think may have been struck on the wrong blank – use accurate scales to check if it weighs less than 5g (the normal weight of a 20p).

5p Coin Hunting

The smallest UK coin denomination in terms of size and weight, so it's not an easy coin to hunt through for errors.

The research test order included a £100 bag of 5p coins, 2000 coins in total were checked for rotation (2008 Shield 5p inverted effigy) and die break errors.

165,172,000 2008 Shield 5ps entered circulation, only 15 were spotted and none had any degree of rotation error.

Note: Coin Reclamation Programme – it is likely that 65% of cupro-nickel 5p and 10p coins have been removed from circulation and recycled. This means that pre 2012 coin circulating mintage for each year could be one third of issued coin numbers. This would include the 2008 inverted effigy 5p rotation error, which could now be 3 times scarcer than it was.

1 Die Break error was found, where the die had broken around the strings of the harp.

Errors like this are very small and barely noticeable, they will not be worth much but are an interesting addition to a collection.

You will need a great deal of patience, nimble fingers and very good eyesight if you plan to hunt through 5p coins!

2p and 1p

The lower denomination "coppers", now made of Copper-plated steel are the coins that most often end up in a jar – one day to be cashed in at a bank or Coinstar machine.

The research test order included no 2p or 1p coins as the bank didn't have any £20 bags available on the day I sent my request.

To be honest, I was not that disappointed, checking 3,000 coins with a face value of £40 filled me with dread – that combined with the fact that there is not really much to look out for, in my opinion your available Coin Hunting time would be better spent on other denominations.

One point of interest which is currently irrelevant due to the 1971 Coinage Act: The value of the metals in 1p and 2p coins made before September 1992 (Bronze: 97% copper, 2.5% zinc, 0.5% tin) is greater than the face value of the coin (perhaps about double) - but Section 10 of the Act means you can't melt them down and sell the scrap metal at this point in time.

The infamous and confusing to many NEW PENCE 1983 2p was only packaged in sets, such as the promotional Martini and Heinz sets shown below.

The 1983 Martini and Heinz Coin Sets
(Images: Michael Coins)

All 2p coins dated between 1971 and 1981 bear the inscription NEW PENCE. From 1982 onwards the inscription was changed to TWO PENCE but a small number of 1983-dated 2p coins were struck in error bearing the old NEW PENCE inscription.

It is therefore only the 1983-dated NEW PENCE coins which are of interest to collectors, it would be extremely unlikely that you would find this coin in circulation.

If in the past, a pack had been opened by someone needing £1.88½p (or 88½p from the Heinz set) – it would still need to be one of the few that contained the error coin for one coin to join many billions in circulation (over 11 billion 2ps have entered circulation since 1971).

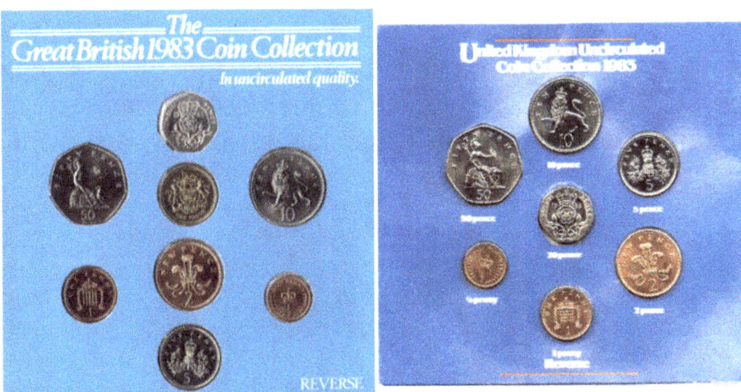

1983 coins in the Martini Set which included a £1 coin and Heinz Set (Images: Michael Coins)

The sets shown above both include the 1983 NEW PENCE 2p, but in the vast majority of Martini and Heinz sets you would find the correct, non error 1983 TWO PENCE version.

Available data suggests that the error coin was present in the Martini set, more often than it was found in the Heinz set.

Today only 23p can still be spent in shops as the round £1, larger 50p / 10p / 5p and ½p have all been demonetised.

Non Royal Mint Coins in UK Circulation

Coins from UK Territories such as Gibraltar and Crown Dependencies like Jersey, Guernsey and the Isle of Man are common in UK circulation.

The coin denominations as well as size and weight are the same as the UK, so whilst they are not legal tender within the UK, it is easy to understand how they enter and stay in circulation.

Coin processing centres are not sophisticated enough to identify these coins, so once in circulation, they move freely through the banking systems to end up in change again and again.

There were two 5p coins from Jersey, one from Guernsey and one 10p from the Isle of Man in the bags of coins ordered as research. Some coins from Territories and Crown Dependencies are collectible and a few are worth a good amount over face value.

Foreign coins of a similar colour, size and weight will also continue to circulate for a while, a significant number of foreign coins are processed as UK coins in cash centres and turn up in bank bags.

There was one foreign coin in the £250 bag of 50p coins ordered as research this book – it was a 2012 2 Franc coin, which is round and weighs a bit more than a 50p at 8.9g.

As this coin can't be spent or paid back into the bank, I can accept the loss, complain to the bank or try to sell it.

The 8 Most Common Non UK 50ps in UK Circulation

These 50p designs tend to sell in the UK for about £2, with the exception of the Gibraltar Bottlenose Dolphins 50p, which is valued at about £4.

There are some rare year dates to look out for:

The Jersey 2003 Grosnez Castle with a mintage of 10,000 would sell for about £70.

The Guernsey 2006 Freesia flowers with a mintage of 22,000 would sell for about £25.

The Gibraltar 1998 and 1999 TT Motorcycle Races would sell for about £50 each.

TT Motorcycle Races

Years of Issue: 1997, **1998**, **1999**
Circulation Mintage: Unknown

Milner's Tower

Years of Issue: 2004 - 2016
Circulation Mintage: Unknown

Loaghtan Ram

Years of Issue: 2017 - 2021
Circulation Mintage: Unknown

Capture of Gibraltar

Years of Issue: 2006 - 2013
Circulation Mintage: Unknown

Bottlenose Dolphins

Years of Issue: 1997 - 2003
Circulation Mintage: Unknown

Barbary Ape

Image: crawleycoins.co.uk

Years of Issue: 2014 - 2016
Circulation Mintage: Unknown

Acknowledgements

I would like to thank everyone who supplied coin images, whether used in this publication or not.

Thank you to NGC for providing a wide variety of UK error coin images from the Beeston Collection. NGC images include all those where a slab holder is visible and those marked with (Image: NGC).

Thank you to The Royal Mint Museum for providing some fascinating and unusual UK error coin images from their own collection, including never before published images. The Royal Mint Museum images include all those on the following pages and those marked with (Image: The Royal Mint Museum). Also acknowledging The Royal Mint for the minting process images and other coin images.

Thank you to the Coin Community including the Facebook Groups: Error Coins & Fakes; Error coins and oddities; with members providing quality images of some stunning UK error coins from their own personal collections. Peter, OZ, Roger, Michael Coins, KBCoins, Crawley Coins, Just Right Collectibles, Darren, Anton, Frank, Gerry, Matt, Lee M.

I would also like to thank everyone who offered expert advice and opinions, including Chris (The Royal Mint Museum), Jamie (NGC), Jason (British Error Coins) and Roger.

Information and Resources: I appreciate the work of all those providing relevant and accurate UK coin information. The source of much of the "unpublished" decimal coin information; Change Range (Lee H) and thanks to Mr Jibble for some interesting insights via your YouTube channel.

The Royal Mint Museum Collection

A selection of coins that never left the factory and did not quite fit into any of the "normal" error categories.

1. Clipped Outer and Offset Inner Blank; 2. Metal Mix Up: Off Metal Outer and Inner; 3. Outer not really struck

Three unusual Struck Through bi-metal coins - where similar struck through items were on both sides of the blank, part covering the centre insert.

The third of the reverse and obverse struck through errors was also struck off metal (inner blank).

Three more oddities, including an extreme 20p

1. May be a hole punched after struck 10p due to the clean shape of the hole; 2. Similar Metal Outer and Inner; 3. ##?!!# the only explanation I can offer is a lump of metal struck with 20p dies (obverse struck through).

Glossary of Terms and Abbreviations

Blank (also called a planchet or flan) - A blank piece of metal prepared to be struck by dies to create a coin.

Alloy – A mixture of metals bound together to create a material fit for the intended purpose. Cupro-nickel is often used for coins, the alloy of Copper and Nickel is strong and resistant to corrosion and germs.

Plated - Plated coins are made from cheaper metals such as steel, then plated in other metals to protect from rusting.

Coining Press - A modern coining press is a machine which creates coins by striking blanks at a rate of up to 850 per minute.

Hopper - A container attached to the top of a coining press to receive blanks, tapers downward to discharge its contents to be fed towards the dies to be struck.

Collar (or retaining collar) - Surrounds the blank to stop metal flowing outward when struck to create a coin with a clean edge.

Edge: Plain / Milled (or Reeded) - The edge of a coin is normally plain (flat) like a 50p or milled with grooved lines as seen on most £2 coins and 10ps.

Struck - The action of striking a metal blank between 2 dies to create a coin.

Die - A hardened metal tool created with a reverse or obverse coin image used to strike an impression onto softer metal.

Reverse - The "tails" side of a coin which may feature a unique design to mark a UK event or achievements of a person.

Obverse - The "heads" side of a coin which would usually feature a portrait of the monarch and may also show the coin year date / denomination.

Denomination - The face value of an individual coin.

Definitive Coin - A general use and standard design (not commemorative) for a given year or period of years.

Commemorative Coin - Created to commemorate something or someone. Such as a UK historical figure or event at a meaningful year date anniversary.

Circulation Coin - A coin struck by The Royal Mint at the request of HM Treasury, to enter UK circulation to fulfil monetary demand. Circulation quality coins are produced quickly and to a lower standard than those made to be sold as collectors items (Brilliant Uncirculated).

Brilliant Uncirculated (BU or BUNC) Coin - A coin struck to a higher standard than circulating coins. Struck multiple times with greater force to give the coin better definition.

Coin Hunting - Checking coins for those of interest, needed for a collection or worth more than face value.

Bank Run - Collecting bags of coins from a bank or Post Office to hunt for coins of interest.

Bank Bag / Post Office Bag (may be prefixed with Full or Large) - A bag prepared for the transport and distribution of coins, containing a fixed amount in value (£s) as small bags of a single denomination.

Sealed Bag - Fixed amount single denomination packs, such as £10 in 50p coins, packaged in heat sealed bags from UK cash centres. Can contain any mix of new release and older coins.

Cud - An area of raised metal on a coin that happens when a damaged die strikes a blank.

We have spent a great deal of time and care in the collation and presentation of information in this book, but please note that inaccuracies, mistakes or omissions may be present.

Coin values presented in this book are guide prices as at the publication date. We can accept no liability for the accuracy of the prices quoted.

All rights reserved. No part of this publication may be reproduced, stored in a retrieval system, or transmitted in any form or by any means, without the prior permission of Coin Hunter Limited.

You can use the Coin Hunter app to find, value and keep track of the coins in your collection. Pictures and information about United Kingdom circulation and Brilliant Uncirculated 50p, £2, A to Z 10p and £5 coins.